Tilting the Continent

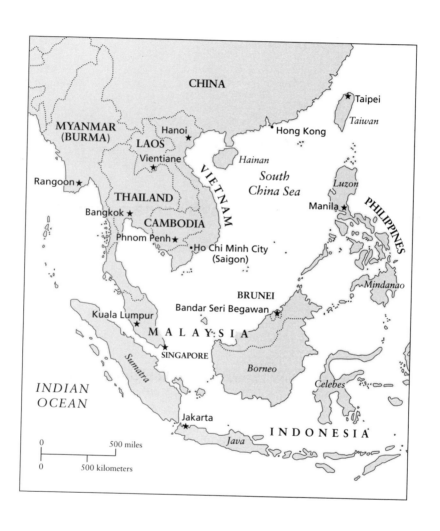

CHINA

MYANMAR
(BURMA)

LAOS

Hanoi ★

Vientiane ★

Rangoon ★

THAILAND

Bangkok ★

CAMBODIA

Phnom Penh ★

Ho Chi Minh City
(Saigon)

VIETNAM

Hainan

South
China Sea

Taipei ★

Taiwan

Hong Kong

Luzon

Manila ★

PHILIPPINES

Mindanao

BRUNEI

Bandar Seri Begawan ★

Kuala Lumpur ★

MALAYSIA

SINGAPORE ★

Sumatra

Borneo

Celebes

INDIAN
OCEAN

Jakarta ★

Java

INDONESIA

0 ____ 500 miles

0 ____ 500 kilometers

TILTING THE CONTINENT

Southeast Asian American Writing

Shirley Geok-lin Lim and Cheng Lok Chua, editors

n
RIVERS
e
PRESS
w

2000

First Edition

Library of Congress Card Catalog Number: 99-68471

ISBN: 0-89823-206-6

Book design and typesetting by Percolator

New Rivers Press is a nonprofit literary press dedicated to publishing emerging writers.

This activity is made possible in part by a grant provided by the Minnesota State Arts Board, through an appropriation by the Minnesota State Legislature. In addition, this activity is supported in part by a grant from the National Endowment for the Arts.

Additional support has been provided by the General Mills Foundation, the McKnight Foundation, the Star Tribune Foundation, and the contributing members of New Rivers Press.

NATIONAL
ENDOWMENT
FOR THE
ARTS

MINNESOTA
STATE ARTS BOARD

New Rivers Press
420 North Fifth Street Suite 1180
Minneapolis, MN 55401

www.newriverspress.org

for Gershom (S.G.L.)
and
Iu-Hui and Poh-Pheng (C.L.C.)

Contents

Returnings

Becoming American

Introduction

Shirley Geok-lin Lim and Cheng Lok Chua

The southeast region of Asia sticks out of the lower right-hand corner of the Asian landmass like a thigh and a foot, with thousands of islands and archipelagoes sprinkled below, crowding the South China Sea and extending into the Pacific Ocean. According to the historian D. G. E. Hall, the term "South-East Asia" became generally used during World War II to cover "the mainland states of Burma, Thailand, Laos, Cambodia, North and South Vietnam and Malaya together with the two great island groups . . . the Republic of Indonesia and the Republic of the Philippines" (3). The history of the region has been one of simultaneous mixing and maintenance of local differences. As Hall notes, "There has obviously been a great deal of intermixture between the earlier inhabitants and later comers. The whole area, indeed, has been described as a chaos of races and languages" (5).

The Southeast Asian region had been traditionally viewed as divided into two cultural spheres, one in which Indian influences predominated (sometimes identified as "Greater India"), and the other, "Greater China," in which Chinese influences ruled. Similarities abound in these countries, separated by seas and borders. They share a similar tropical or subtropical climate, flora, and fauna. In many places, societies possess a kinship system based on strong family and community bonds and uphold East Asian Confucian values. Together, their common histories include Hindu, Buddhist, and Muslim, as well as Christian, influences and a syncretic approach to multiple cultural and racial crossings.

Geographically, however, the region is characterized by a tremendous variety of indigenous peoples, languages, and cultures. Distinct tribes and political systems dominate territories that are separated physically by rivers, mountains, and seas, as well as by linguistic, religious, and social differences. This tendency to fragmentation was exacerbated by the actions of Western colonial powers. Beginning as early as the fifteenth century, Portugal and Spain, and later Holland, England, and the United States, seized much of this territory for markets and resources, and imposed dissimilar Western cultural and language policies on adjacent lands. Buddhist Thailand remained an independent state throughout the period of Western colonization, while the British colonized Burma, now known as Myanmar. The countries of Vietnam, Laos, and Cambodia, colonized by the French as "Indochina," share a francophone colonial history; emerging from years of internal conflict and wars with Western nations, including the United States, these countries are now rapidly modernizing toward a globalizing anglophone present. These states on the mainland of the continent are seldom confused with Indonesia, a nation composed of thousands of islands, colonized by Holland and now a secular state with a large Muslim majority. Nor does Malaysia, a post-British colony with a Muslim-dominant but multi-racial population, resemble the Philippines, a majority-Christian independent state that was colonized by both Spain and the United States. Brunei, now independent of British sovereignty and blessed with vast oil reserves, remains a stable society, significantly wealthier than its neighbors.

Today, Southeast Asian nations are looking for a shared identity and destiny without, however, sacrificing their political and cultural autonomy. ASEAN, the Association of Southeast Asian Nations, inaugurated in 1967, has helped create a regional identity based on common security and economic goals (Sandhu xiii–xvi). The ten member states of ASEAN are Brunei, Cambodia, Indonesia, Laos, Malaysia, Myanmar, the Philippines, Singapore, Thailand, and Vietnam. Together, the population of Southeast Asia is almost five hundred million, and its total economy equals nine-tenths that of China, the most populous nation in the world (Commonwealth of Australia 9).

In crossing over to the United States of America, immigrants from Southeast Asia carry with them their multicultural histories, histories that are peculiarly resonant with contemporary social and cultural phenomena in late-twentieth-century America. But it is these very multicultural strains that have made Americans of Southeast Asian descent less visible, not only in the mainstream of American society, but also in the consciousness of the ethnic community now recognized as "Asian Americans." A number of excellent anthologies on the writing of specific national-descent groups have already appeared. For example, Nick Carbo, *Returning a Borrowed Tongue* (1995), focuses on Filipino American authors, while Tran, Truong, and Khoi, *Watermark: Vietnamese American Poetry and Prose* (1997), includes only Vietnamese American writing. The present volume, *Tilting the Continent*, is the first anthology of Southeast Asian American writing to be published. It foregrounds and privileges the writing of Americans from the entire region of Southeast Asia. By gathering these stories, poems, and essays into a collectivity, we hope that they will illuminate each other. In bringing together the writing of American writers who are of Southeast Asian origin, we hope to make emphatic the voices of these new Americans. They speak from shared experiences, as refugees, as first-generation immigrants moving from a colonial history to a postcolonial present, with common social, political, and cultural concerns and traditions. Southeast Asian Americans have come from a region that is a "chaos of races and languages," entering an American nation that is itself a crucible of races and languages. The writing in these pages testifies to the emergence of Southeast Asian American literature written in English. Other languages—Thai, Cambodian, and so on—form a communal well whose water nourishes the imagination, and in whose depths cultural traces and memories are suspended.

◆ ◆ ◆

Southeast Asian Americans, like Euro-Americans, are either immigrants or descendants of immigrants. The 1990 census counted more than 2.5 million Southeast Asian Americans, who thus formed the largest bloc of Asian Americans, outnumbering the 1.64 million Chinese Americans (Anderson and Walker 6). It may further surprise some readers to learn that Southeast Asians have been coming to the Americas since the sixteenth century. When Spain colonized Mexico, it also colonized the Philippines (named for Philip II), and the Manila galleon trade flourished between the Philippines and Mexico from 1565 to 1815. In 1763 (even before the American colonists broke away from the British), a band of Filipinos rebelled against their oppressive Spanish masters in Mexico and migrated to Barataria Bay in Louisiana, thirty miles from New Orleans. There they constructed a Southeast Asian–style fishing village on stilts (Chan 25); and some of these Filipinos fought against the British and alongside Jean Lafitte (whose stronghold was in Barataria Bay) during the Battle of New Orleans in 1815 (Gall and Natividad 175). It is also noteworthy that in California in 1781, when the little Pueblo de Nuestra Señora Reina de los Angeles was founded by forty-six settlers, there was among them a Filipino named Antonio Miranda (Gall and Natividad 175). That little pueblo is now known as Los Angeles.

After these modest beginnings, the immigration of Southeast Asians to America rose dramatically during three historical time periods. Two of them occurred on the heels of American political and military involvement in Southeast Asia. One of these followed upon the Spanish-American War of 1898, when the American dream of westward expansion and predestined empire reached out into the Pacific to embrace the then Spanish colony of the Philippines. The other began on April 29–30, 1975, when 86,000 South Vietnamese refugees were airlifted from their homeland in the wake of the failure of American military and political strategy after the decade-long Vietnam War against the North Vietnam–led Communists (Takaki 449; Wieder 165). Yet another historical time period followed upon the relaxation of anti-Asian U.S. immigration laws, after the 1965 Immigration Act removed "national origin" as a basis for immigration quotas and allowed for family reunification (Chan 145).

The Spanish-American War involved the Philippines, which, at the outbreak of hostilities in 1898, had been a colony of Spain for four centuries. On May 1, Admiral George Dewey led the U.S. Asiatic squadron into Manila Bay and defeated the Spanish flotilla without a single casualty. Dewey also brought with him Emilio Aguinaldo, a Filipino nationalist leader of Chinese and Tagalog ancestry whom the Spanish had exiled to Hong Kong in 1897. Aguinaldo resumed his struggle for Filipino independence, allied his ground forces with Dewey's, and defeated the Spanish. On June 12 (celebrated as Independence Day), the Filipinos declared their independence and began setting up their own government with Aguinaldo as its president. However, in the Treaty of Paris, signed in December 1898, Spain ceded the Philippines to the United States, and the Filipinos then had to fight a bloody guerrilla war against the Americans, their former allies now become their masters. After casualties estimated in the hundreds of thousands, Aguinaldo was captured by the Americans in 1901, and the Filipino resistance wound down (Chan 17; San Juan 2).

With the American annexation of the Philippines, a modest number of Filipino students (*pensionados*) were sent to the United States for education and returned to their native land to positions of influence and affluence (Melegrito 73). However, the Philippine annexation came at a time when cheap Asian labor was dwindling because of the Chinese Exclusion Act (1882) and the Gentlemen's Agreement with Japan (1907). Because of their colonial status, Filipinos were "American nationals" (though not full-fledged American citizens), and thus exempt from exclusionary immigration laws. Hence Filipinos began to be extensively recruited as cheap labor for American agriculture. From 1911 to 1920, 869 Filipinos immigrated to the United States; from 1921 to 1930, this figure grew to 54,747 (Melegrito 65). Immigration to Hawaii was even more dramatic: during 1907–1929, 71,594 Filipinos were brought to work in the cane fields there, and in 1920 Filipinos already accounted for 30 percent of all plantation workers in Hawaii.

Since that initial surge, Filipino immigration has had its ups and downs. During the Great Depression of the 1930s, the United States decided to close its gates to the immigration of these Asians. The 1934 Tydings-McDuffie Independence Act created the Commonwealth of the Philippines, whereby the Philippines could then be considered a "separate country" and allocated a quota of fifty immigrants into the United States per year (Melegrito 75). However, during World War II, Filipinos and Americans became comrades in arms fighting the Japanese invasion of the Philippines. Thus in the decade following World War II, 19,307 Filipinos immigrated to the United States.

Another dramatic influx of Southeast Asians into America originated from the countries of the Indochinese peninsula and came about as a result of the American political and military intervention called the Vietnam War. In fact, the Vietnam War was part of the three decades of almost endless combat that ravaged this region after World War II. From 1946 to 1954, the nationalist Vietminh, under the leadership of Ho Chi Minh, fought for independence from their former colonial masters, the French. After the defeat of the French at Dien Bien Phu, the 1954 Geneva Accords partitioned Vietnam into a pro-Communist North and an anti-Communist South. North Vietnam attempted to reunify the country by launching a guerrilla war in the South. Fearing that the neighboring Southeast Asian nations would fall into Communist hands (like dominoes) if South Vietnam were to become Communist, the United States intervened (Ng 1612–13). At first, American military advisers were dispatched. Then, in 1965, U.S. combat troops were sent. By 1968, American troop strength had reached 540,000 (Karnow 682). But the North Vietnamese proved to be tenacious, and Americans at home protested the continuation of U.S. military involvement, so American troops began to be withdrawn in 1969.

When Americans gave up the Vietnam War and fled from Saigon (now Ho Chi Minh City) on April 30, 1975, hundreds of thousands of South Vietnamese, Hmong, Laotians, and Cambodians who had allied themselves with Americans became endangered refugees and sought sanctuary in the United States. Many fled on foot through perilous jungles to transit refugee camps set up in Thailand whence they might be airlifted to Guam and then to the American mainland. Others stole away by boat into the South China Sea, braving pirates and the elements, in hopes of being picked up by American vessels or of making landfall in a neighboring non-Communist country. (These latter refugees came to be known as "boat people.") By 1989, more than 1.5 million people had left Southeast Asia, many finding their way to the United States. According to the U.S. Department of Health, Education, and Welfare, 1,085,612 refugees from Southeast Asia had been settled in the United States between 1975 and 1992 (Gall and Natividad 319). Of these refugees, as could be expected, the Vietnamese were the most numerous. In 1991, there were an estimated 850,000 Vietnamese in the United States (Wieder 165). The Hmong people, mostly originating from Laos, and having been trained into a surrogate fighting force by the CIA, also became refugees after almost two-thirds of their population died either from starvation or warfare (Bankston 81). About 95,000 Hmong had settled in the United States by 1990. A similar exodus from Pathet Lao–controlled Laos is recorded, and the 1990 census counts about 150,000 Laotian Americans (excluding the Hmong); an equivalent number of Cambodian Americans fled Pol Pot's killing fields (Gall and Gall 451).

Much less traumatic has been the immigration of Southeast Asian Americans that burgeoned after the 1965 Immigration Act and its amendments (Chan 145). Ever since the Chinese Exclusion

Act of 1882, the race-based immigration laws of the United States had sought to prevent Asian immigration into America. But in 1962, President Kennedy urged Congress "to correct the mistakes of the past," and the Immigration and Nationality Act of 1965 did away with race as a criterion for immigration (Kingston 158). This and subsequent immigration reforms also allowed U.S. citizens and residents to bring over relatives under a family reunification statute.

The Southeast Asian American group that grew the most noticeably under these new laws was the Filipinos. For instance, 19,307 Filipinos immigrated to the U.S. between 1951 and 1960; between 1961 and 1970, this number grew to 98,376; to 360,216 between 1971 and 1980; and to 495,278 between 1981 and 1990 (Melegrito 65). In 1990, Filipino Americans totaled 1,406,770 (Anderson and Walker 7).

Thai, Indonesian, Burmese, Malaysian, and other Southeast Asians also began to migrate into the United States under the post-1960s immigration statutes. These Southeast Asian Americans have settled in the United States because of marriage (or other family-related reasons), for economic opportunity, or for educational advancement. For instance, the immigration of Thais to the United States was nearly nonexistent before 1960, but as Thailand became the rest-and-recreation resort for U.S. service personnel stationed in Vietnam, Thais intermarried with and worked for Americans, who made them aware of the attractions of life in America. By 1990, there were approximately 91,275 Americans of Thai ancestry in America (Gall and Natividad 159). Similarly, 30,085 Indonesians had settled in America by 1990 (Gall and Natividad 95). And during the decade of 1981-1991, 10,180 Burmese, 13,134 Malaysians, and 5,159 Singaporeans immigrated to the United States (Gall and Gall 516–17).

◆ ◆ ◆

Like many other immigrant literatures, Southeast Asian American writing appears heavily focused on expressions of the immigration experience. But immigrant history and experiences are different for each national and ethnic group and for individual authors. Often these experiences are narrated through autobiographical poetry, memoirs, and creative nonfiction. These writings offer themes and possess cultural presences different from those portrayed in Euro-American literature as well as in many Asian American works published before 1970.

Some of the best examples of Filipino American writing, however, appeared just after World War II. Carlos Bulosan's *America Is in the Heart*, subtitled *A Personal History*, appeared first in 1943. Bulosan (1913–1956) was a prolific writer, and although he died of tuberculosis at the early age of forty-three, he left behind a rich collection of poems, stories, essays, and memoirs. Many of Bienvenido N. Santos's and N. V. M. Gonzalez's stories and novels dealt with Filipino experiences in the United States but were published first in the Philippines. Santos's collection of stories *Scent of Apples*, for example, appeared in the United States in 1979, although the title story was published in Manila in 1948. By the 1980s, Filipino-born writers such as Jessica Hagedorn and Ninotchka Rosca began to be read within an American cultural framework even though their books may be set in the Philippines. Unlike an earlier generation, Filipino American authors in this anthology—Joseph 0. Legaspi, Vince Gotera, Ruth Pe Palileo, Oliver de la Paz, Noel Alumit, Eugene Gloria, Marianne Villanueva, Nick Carbo, Geronimo G. Tagatac, M. G. Sorongon, Anna Alves, and Paulino Lim Jr.—identify themselves as Filipino American, no matter their place of birth. Despite their U.S. residence, their writings often share a common imagined tropical landscape. This lush imagery and a strong valuation of family and community are elements that pervade Southeast Asian American literature.

Filipino Americans have had a longer apprenticeship in the English language, for the American colonialists brought U.S.-style education with them to the islands after the U.S. annexation of the Philippines in 1901. Later Southeast Asian immigrants generally arrived with less command of English. The narrators or characters in the contributions by Vietnamese, Cambodian, Hmong, and Thai writers may often portray recently arrived refugees and immigrants who handle the English language with different accents. Their narratives and poems may be marked by qualities of oral speech and Asian-inflected stylistic registers. Such subtle shadings can be found in the work of Lan Duong, Minh-Mai Hoang, Jora Trang, Chachoua Victoria Xiong, Kay Vu-Lee, U Sam Oeur, Jade Quang Huynh, and Pornsak Pichetshote.

Writers from post-British-colonial societies—Shirley Lim, Fiona Cheong, Hilary Tham, Mahani Zubaidy, and BeeBee Tan-Beck, for example—have a different relationship to English and to English-dominant U.S. culture. Their works possess a literary reflexivity, allusiveness, and consciousness that mark them as coming from a more English-language-based, albeit British, colonial tradition. Shirley Lim, who was schooled in British Malaya had already published several books in English overseas prior to being published in the United States. For example, her first book of poems, *Crossing the Peninsula* (1980), garnered the (British) Commonwealth Poetry Prize, and her 1989 collection of poems, *Modern Secrets,* was published in Australia. Recognized for their poetic exploration of the ironies of finding a voice in a borrowed tongue, the disorientation of living with each foot in a different culture, and the travail of actualizing a female self in a male-dominated society, Lim's American-published books have also won U.S. literary prizes: the American Book Award for the coedited anthology *The Forbidden Stitch: An Asian American Woman's Anthology* (1989), and again for her memoir, *Among the White Moon Faces* (1996). Similarly, Fiona Cheong, who grew up in post-British-colonial Singapore, published a well-reviewed first novel, *The Scent of the Gods,* in 1991, and is represented in these pages by a finely crafted excerpt from a work in progress. Although not represented in this volume, mention must be made of the Burmese American refugee Wendy Law-Yone (whose father edited the leading English-language newspaper of British colonial Burma); her first novel, *The Coffin Tree* (1983), was very well received as a sensitive portrayal of mental illness in a Southeast Asian immigrant, and her second novel, *Irrawaddy Tango* (1993), is an ingenious bricolage of American pop culture artifacts. Also noteworthy but not included here is the Indonesian-born poet Li-Young Lee, who came to the United States by way of British-ruled Hong Kong. His first book of intensely felt, brooding poems, *Rose* (1986), was greeted with critical acclaim; his second, *The City in Which I Love You* (1990), won the Lamont Award of the Academy of American Poets; and his memoir, *The Winged Seed: A Remembrance* (1995), is a hauntingly oneiric book.

Together, Southeast Asian American writing can be said to tilt Asian American and mainstream American literature in a new and different direction. This anthology reminds us of a Southeast Asian past and present composed of polyethnic, multilingual, and rapidly modernizing societies. But it is also an inherently American phenomenon, a demonstration of writing as U.S. culture making, and a drawing together of some of the newest immigrant writers to the United States to offer an original collective perspective and voice.

Works Cited

Anderson, Patrick, and Brad Walker, eds. *Asians in America: 1990* Census. San Francisco: Asian Week, 1991.

Bankston, Carl L., III. "Who Are the Hmong Americans?" *The Asian American Almanac.* Ed. Susan Gall and Irene Natividad. Detroit: Gale Research, 1995. 81–89.

Carbo, Nick, ed. *Returning a Borrowed Tongue: Poems by Filipino and Filipino American Writers.* Minneapolis: Coffee House Press, 1996.

Chan, Sucheng. *Asian Americans: An Interpretive History.* Boston: Twayne, 1991.

Commonwealth of Australia, Department of Foreign Affairs and Trade. *The New ASEANS: Vietnam, Burma, Cambodia and Laos.* Barton, ACT: BHP, 1997.

Gall, Susan, and Timothy Gall. *Statistical Record of Asian Americans.* Detroit: Gale Research, 1993.

Gall, Susan, and Irene Natividad, eds. *The Asian American Almanac.* Detroit: Gale Research, 1995.

Hall, D. G. E. *A History of South-East Asia.* 1955. London: Macmillan, 1981.

Karnow, Stanley. *Vietnam: A History.* New York: Viking, 1983.

Kingston, Maxine Hong. *China Men.* New York: Knopf, 1980

Melegrito, Jonathan. "Who Are the Filipino Americans?" *The Asian American Almanac.* Ed. Susan Gall and Irene Natividad. Detroit: Gale Research, 1995. 63–80.

Ng, Franklin, ed. *Asian American Encyclopedia.* New York: Michael Cavendish, 1995.

Sandhu, K. S. "Preface." *The ASEAN Reader,* ed. K. S. Sandhu et al. Singapore: Institute of Southeast Asian Studies 1992. xiii–xvi.

San Juan, E., Jr. "One Hundred Years of Producing and Reproducing the 'Filipino.'" *Amerasia Journal* 24.2 (1998), 1–33.

Takaki, Ronald. *Strangers from a Different Shore.* Boston: Little, Brown, 1989.

Tran, Barbara, Monique T. D. Truong, and Luu Truong Khoi, eds. *Watermark: Vietnamese American Poetry and Prose.* New York: Asian American Writers' Workshop, 1997.

Wieder, Rosalie. "Who Are the Vietnamese Americans?" *The Asian American Almanac.* Ed. Susan Gall and Irene Natividad. Detroit: Gale Research, 1995. 165–174.

Family

The Immigrants' Son

Joseph O. Legaspi

In my house, nuzzled in leafy suburbia,
ants nest on the chinaware and chip away
the designs; seafood remains frostbitten
in the freezer; pubic hair thrives under the dampness
of mats and towels; my grandmother's overripe
bitter squashes burst in the backyard,
dropping to the ground, uneaten.

I give you my mother,
mourning our adulthoods
like any other deaths.
She holds nightly vigils
watching shows she doesn't care for.
Forget it. She has given up on prayers;
she doesn't read books. She worries
about her sons chasing white women,
about her daughters being chased
by white men, or worse, black men.
My mother misses the splintered Old World
house where my grandmother resided
upstairs with her unmarried children
and in the apartment rooms below lived
her married children and their children,
families sleeping side by side
on beds pushed together,
dreaming of the archipelago.

And I give you a memory
of that year when my aunt gave birth
to her firstborn, twin stillborn boys,
grayish, mummified cupids.
They were placed in a pickled egg jar
and buried in the dark, musty earth
beneath our protruding house,
creaking heavily under too much weight.

Looking out of a window to our backyard,
leaning on a weakened wall, caressing
the throbbing aliveness of a splinter
in the palm of my hand, I wonder
whether I would find the jar half-filled with
brittle baby bones
if I dug deep enough where
the next overripe bitter squash falls.

The Mother

Joseph O. Legaspi

She took away the crayons and washed
the walls until they were white again.
My mother gave me old newspapers to play with.
My hands itched. I tore
at the gray papers, first, in anger, forming
undefined shapes, later, in increasing amusement,
more intricate two-dimensional figures—
the world taken out of the walls.
For years then I drew out of the rectangles the contours
of elephants, *carabaos,* and people.
I ripped a herd of Appaloosas;
tended to the lacerated bodies of my soldiers;
shredded rain for my reenactment of Noah's Ark.
On the end of each paper-cutting day, my mother
collected the discarded pieces of newspaper
and wiped my hands and face,
tenderly, with a warm towel.
What was she washing away from my skin?
One afternoon, the smudged towel hung
from a chair and I looked at my right hand.
On my thumb, a toppled *a,* a trapped snail;
a splinter of an *i;* a fading *k.*
On my other fingers, the *b, d,* and *p* assembled
like musical notes; the hairs on the *o;*
the conjunction *ng,* a bridge.
I licked my thumb, pressed it on the wall,
and the *a* stayed. Twice more
until I spelled *ako:* me, in Tagalog.
I turned around and saw my mother,
her hands on her waist.
She left the room, returning with a pencil and a notebook—clean,
lined paper—and we sat down,
my mother showing me the way
as I rest my thumb on the pencil buttressed
by my finger where a corn will bloom.

Killing a Chicken

Joseph O. Legaspi

My mother killed chickens,
making the same crisp sound
of separation: a guava from its stem,
a fowl's breakage from its life.

I liked chickens enough; I respected them.
My roosters had names: *Kukoro, Loro, Talisayin.*
But my romance with them was a detachable bridge.
When served to us fried, garnished in
garlic, or in stew, my siblings and I would just
exclaim how tasty *Kukoro* was.

Weeks after my ninth birthday, while feeding
the chickens worms I gathered from a ditch,
my uncle's shadow engulfed me, his hand
rubbed my hair as he entered the coop in a gust
of feathers and dust. He brought out a plain
white hen, one unnamed because she was unappealing,
too common in her whiteness—a finch, a house lizard.
I followed my uncle to the cold cement steps.
Sitting down, he tucked the chicken between
his thighs, its head drawn back, neck exposed
for plucking. Nearby: a pot full of water
over burning firewood, a pear-shaped bowl.
My uncle smiled, his hand beckoned me to him.
He handed me a razor, the kind for shaving. I took it.
He presented me with the tender, plucked neck.
My hand like steel. I rocked back and forth.
The razor sliced smoothly,
with sincere grace.

The hen quivered, but it was not her life
I was thinking of, it was my mother's:
the life she had given up for her children,
the many deaths she performed, the hearts
and gizzards she had eaten. The liver. It is harder
for a mother, a giver of life, one
who carries an egg-filled nest in her body,
to take a life as I had done with ease,
the fire crackling behind me, the razor
as warm in my hand as the blood
trickling into the bowl.

Christmas '95

Isabelle Thuy Pelaud

Mother. Water pouring from your faucet, too strong, too loud, hard splashes clashing with a porcelain-like sink. Prickly daughter of yours, watching you from a spinning chair across the room. I look through the rectangle made by the counter and the pillar on the right, a large and perfect frame, an image I can only watch, inaccessible from where I stand. For I was asked to sit by my father, his friend, and my husband, to translate. To translate the stories of two Frenchmen reminiscing of a life of another time, a space where they were the center, served, free riders on their mother country, with oh, so proper manners! To translate a time in which they were kings in Vietnam, now, a maneuvering to be continued. There are such things as free rides, you know. Colonial leftovers are thus preserved, passed on, rehearsed into normality.

I scrutinize the details of my fork turning in between my fingers and take refuge behind my education, fast provider of tools to dissect, chop, and unveil, nearly comfortable. But I also see from the corner of my eye that my father, once a young man growing up in a poor family, is a man of principles. He is like his father, who was a man of even stronger principles, a man of the Resistance, untainted, who could shut, with a slam of grandeur, the doors of opportunities his son had opened for himself. "My son shall never be a bourgeois," my grandfather yelled. At least this is how the story goes. To be poor in a French village is boring, stifling, agonizing, petrifying all right. I *know* that. So my father left, left for the taste of adventure, for the savor of a better life in a country far away with the scent of exoticism, a suitcase filled with exuberant fantasies held firmly between his legs. But wouldn't I make similar choices if I had been in his place? And what if my father one day had not made a bet with a colleague that a Frenchman could sweep away the soul and body of a "real" traditional Vietnamese woman? Maybe I, too, would have been born a bit later with a Vietnamese father "gone with the war," but on solid ground. Maybe then I would have fought in a guerrilla platoon.

Mother, you tell me that one day you suddenly changed your major from mathematics to philosophy because of a teacher's words describing the blue transparency of the Mediterranean, the cold and noble marble of Greek colonnades, the scent of lavender sensually licking the hills of the south of France. "I liked dreaming of other worlds," you say. You were the quietest and most invisible one among your seven sisters. You were the good girl that no one worried about. Left alone, you waited for your father, who only came home, it seems, to destroy your mother's business and conceive another child. But your father had a charming smile, a mysterious smile that only those living on the other side of the walls of the courtyard in which you were preciously guarded could make. Your father worked for years in a French bank but, since he had been laid off, could not find a place in a society changing at a pace beyond his comprehension. You thought you could understand him. In spite of the pains he caused your mother, you kept looking for his smile in other men, carrier of nonsaturated air and false promises. And this is how, one day, you simply disappeared. No one predicted what was immediately called your "betrayal" and later on your "love," for your French teacher, whose main asset was Frenchness and a ravishing smile.

As a teenager, I ran out of air to breathe under the relentless violence of French gazes. And if only it was for their gazes alone. Their acts, their words, and the odor of lavender obstructed my pores, causing nausea and dreams of escape. So I ran away to "Little Saigon," California, where my aunt had arrived ten years before because of a war I had seen in passing through a black-and-white TV screen. In her home, I felt accepted for the first time and held on to her blouse as if it were a life preserver sent through space. Calling me an idealist, she threw away my French history book and my used copy of *Das Kapital,* taking time in between two jobs to warn me against sweet words of communism and the lies she saw inscribed inside their songs.

Eleven years later it took only two hours to drive from her house to my parents' house, where I am today, translating my father's voice, watching in between intervals my mother clattering dishes, her eyes fixed to the bottom of a porcelain-like sink. To my surprise, she had succeeded in convincing my father to move to California. Thirty years older than her and now an old man, he cannot take the risk of living alone. My mother and her sisters are cooking. My aunts are passing food across the counter to their husbands, three

Vietnamese American men eating quietly. From my seat, I see three backs curved, bending over three hot bowls of soup. "Please, come sit with us," I say, trying unconvincingly to cross over a gap that should belong to another time. "It's okay, it's okay," one of my uncles responds, brushing his hand in the air, and then distracting himself by looking at his kids, who are watching, bored out of their minds, a video of religious Master Ching Hai, chanting what sounds like love songs. My uncle, too, is waiting, waiting to leave my mother's world and return to his home in Orange County. There, he will sit at the center table with his male friends, loud, waiting to be served by his wife. "It's okay, it's okay." What I hear is that it is okay to go on and to translate the good old colonial tales, maintain the old order, and close my lips. Peace is priceless, after all. And, perhaps, habits coalesced with civilities and stories of the past are just too effective and powerful to breach.

This year, my family is spending Christmas for the first time in Rainbow, California, like in an awkward crystal sea urchin sparkling under an indifferent sun. I am spinning inside its shell, whether I want to or not. The only room available belongs to the realm of daydreams. Lost in my absence, I am yet intermittently awakened by a voice, whispering in my ears across melding clouds piled on top of each other that my ability to plunge eyes-wide-open amidst their boundless forms is not accidental, but due to the privilege and curse of living "in between." *Stillness of the immutable, the unbearable, the so-called natural order of things, centuries of training, infliction of pain, tears, and legacies. Now soft marshes to stand on. In silence, we see, react, unact, and go on with our respective destinies, each of us holding firmly on to our masks. Each carrying more than one. Lips doing the talking, ears doing the listening. Eyes doing.* Tensions I cannot bear but cannot shake. I look at the kids on my right. They are watching an "American Buddha," a daring woman wearing a ten-thousand-dollar dress preaching about spiritual liberation. They, too, are waiting for the time to go home and watch MTV. Behind them, the voices of two old Frenchmen holding on to a past regurgitated to oblivion are mere hubbub.

Everyone in the room is waiting, except for my mother and my aunts, who live in the tempo of the now, hurrying through the chores necessary to maintain the equilibrium of the moment. They are talking in a language I cannot translate, laughing, and passing Chinese microwave Christmas goodies to their people. The faucet stops running. My mother walks to her room. There she will wrap old tennis trophies with "Tom," "Bill," and "John" engraved on golden plates, garage sale finds and gifts to all the men in her life, young and old, patiently waiting to be served but with the certainty that nothing will be ready on time.

My Mother
Is Bui Doi

Lan Duong

Her brown-
sweatered torso
lies
in front of me
on the single bed
she has claimed
hers
for the next three
months.
My mother is *bui doi*
she likes to leave—
di lang thang,
my sisters tell me.

I fumble with her tunic
with hands that are like
broken scissors
in the kitchen.
I bunch the thick knit
up and around
her neck.
The skin has collapsed
like heavy socks.

Her back is
wide and clean
like a cutting board.
My sisters tell me
that she once had
pustules of acne
that were like
strands of pearls

she has
lovingly
passed down
to her daughters.

They tell me that she has
wandered around villages,
gambled, burned money
without prayers,
on solid legs
that did not lend
her any roots.
Now her back
shows only
traces
of fight,
faint scars
like bird tracks
in the dust.
And though
my mother is *bui doi,*
she no longer has
the anger of *ot*
as she waits for me
to push the ache away
from her body.
With her slippers
the color of sky
underneath the bed,
she waits for me,
a weary bride.

This Face

Joseph O. Legaspi

Eyes like magpies in milk,
the caves of the nose, lips,
the darker petals of pink roses;
it is a face of an Asian
derived from the Malays, the hunters in Java, the ancient Chinese
cooling themselves on the banks of the Yangtze,
it is my father's face.

Asian men: in America it could be
another word for mule,
the sterile,
almost female,
the *gook, nips,* and *flips*
who cook beautiful meals with bean sprouts,
cashews, and water chestnuts;
who slice their meats in slivers;
who eat food with sticks like slender fingers;
who do laundry for a living;
who are passive;
who are more cerebral than sexual,
who are prisoners of their genetics:
the undersized, soft frame, bodies almost hairless,
the features of the Mongoloid.

I see the face that looks back at me:
the porcupined eyebrows,
the furrows of the forehead,
the overbite. Same as when I hunch
over a basin of water,
as when I close my eyes to sleep—
it is the face of someone
who favors potatoes;
who has had many affairs with women;
who is the source of my conceit, my Asianness,
my maleness. It is my father's
and I love it.

Father's Duties

Cuong H. Lam

His way was with silence. His words never spoke to us the way his silence did. That blank stare into the nothingness ahead and his closed mouth made the walk home from Grandmother's house cold even in June's rays of pounding light. It scared us to see him this way: lips pressed, eyes bereft, and body barely walking. But there was nothing we could do, there was nothing we could say. We followed his steps with our arms quietly, unmovingly close to our bodies; not making a single sound, like we knew we should. I looked at my brother and sister—he with a note from school pinned to his shirt and she with a rose petal cutout from a cereal box—and I wondered what they were thinking. We knew what his wordlessness meant; it always meant the same thing. What was hinted was always clear.

Our home was located behind an alley. We lived in this house; one bedroom, not big enough for a family to live in. He led us through the dirt alley; his big steps still sent scatters of dust toward us. When he unlocked the door, he made no attempt to direct us in. He pushed the door opened, his right hand resting on the frame, and waited for his children to enter. We stood there and knew that his hand on the doorknob and his barren stare into the house meant for us to enter quietly. The three of us went in one by one, our arms still by our sides, like soldiers marching without a beat. We sat down on the carpeted floor and began to take our shoes off, rolling our socks into balls before stuffing them into our shoes. He followed us in, closed the door behind him and twisted the lock.

My brother and sister ran to the TV and turned it on. As the gray fuzz turned into bright pictures, they stumbled backward onto our sofa, which we had salvaged on a Thursday evening because trash pickups were on Fridays. I watched them sit down as my father walked into the kitchen. When he returned from the kitchen, he stood next to the TV in the doorframe between the kitchen and living room. And what he lacked, he made up for in presence. His simple stance drowned out our world of TV, and all that was in front of us was our father. In his right hand he gripped the feather end of the duster. His hand wrapped around the feathers and slightly bounced

16

the bamboo off his left hand. We looked up at our father, his shadow towered over us.

"Turn off the TV," he said.

We were right in front of him and he revealed nothing with his eyes or face or breath. He didn't see us. It was what made his words even more forceful. We looked at each other, the impact of his silence and words quieted our voices. I walked toward the TV and turned it off.

"Lie down on the floor," he ordered.

We went slowly to the middle of the living room and lay down with our faces in the carpet. Three bodies spread out at our father's feet. I didn't hear him draw the feather duster back, but I heard it whipping through the air and knew it was coming down on me. I held my breath and felt the bamboo stick on my behind. Again, I didn't hear him raise the bamboo stick, but I heard its movement.

Two.

"Ahh!" I let out.

Three.

I began to sob.

Four, five.

I didn't feel it anymore.

Then it was my brother's turn. I didn't look up; my arms had surrounded my sobbing face in the carpet. When I heard the bamboo stick against my brother, I squeezed my eyes tighter trying to block his screams from coming into my ears. It didn't work, I kept hearing the bamboo whipping and then his screams. Again, it was a rush of air, followed by the lashing of flesh and the loud cry. Three. Lash of flesh. Four. Scream. Five. It was over for my brother, and his cries between quick breaths made me cry even harder.

He must've walked over to my sister. Our cries muffled the creaking of wood from his steps. But we heard the bamboo stick striking through the air, meeting flesh, and then our sister's cries. We squeezed our eyes harder and held our breaths, trying to block out her pleas. This we could not do.

Two.

"It hurts a lot," she pleaded in Vietnamese.

Three.

"Ba! Ba, what are you doing?"

17

Four.

"*Ba!* It hurts a lot. *Ba!*" she cried.

Five.

Her sobs became wailing screams.

When he finished what he had started, my father left the living room. We all knew it was over and we slowly crept up. I watched my brother sit up with his legs spread open and hands grabbing the carpet, trying to rip it out. My sister sat up, her body slouched and arms between her legs, the rose petal cutout crumpled in her small fingers. I watched them both.

We sat there crying our anger out. The gray television screen stared at us. In the reflection we saw each other cry. We stared. Our quick, short breaths slowly retreated into slow, quiet breaths. Our anger was gone, we didn't remember.

I turned on the TV again and we all sat back down on the sofa: myself, my brother and my sister. Our order not only marked the order of our birth, it defined our priorities to each other and our responsibilities to our parents. We knew that everything came down to it—from who got things first to who got punished first. Their tears were my responsibility, I knew that. I watched, I had to. Through their nearly dried eyes, we escaped and forgot.

"Drink your milk," my father ordered from the kitchen.

We walked into the kitchen to find our usual cups of milk on the small table next to the gallons of water and cereal boxes. An orange cup in each of our hands, we drank our daily dose of milk and showed our father that we were good by quickly finishing it. We showed him our empty cups proudly. He nodded.

When Mom comes home from work we'll tell her how quickly we finished our milk, we told him. Again he nodded. His work was not done, he was still cleaning the rice for dinner. And he had the cups to wash. We returned to our TV. It made us forget.

"Cuong, come in and take your bath," my father called from the bathroom.

I entered the bathroom and saw my father's hand under the running water, making sure the water wasn't too hot or too cold. He helped me remove my clothes and I climbed into the tub. I watched my father as he washed me with his hands, cleaning with water.

"You see," he said, staring at my burning red marks, "you're so disobedient."

I didn't say anything.

"Khiem and Mui, come here at look at your brother's disobedience," he ordered.

My brother and sister entered the bathroom and he made me turn around so that they could see all the red marks on my behind. They looked at the marks as if they didn't know what had happened. And when he told them they could leave, they walked outside to the sound of the TV. With a towel, my father gently dried me and handed me a small yellow comb.

"Here, comb your hair," he said.

As he pushed the door open, I walked through. He stood there in the doorway and reminded my brother and sister that he was their father.

"Did you two see that? It's what happens to you when you're disobedient," he told them.

They knew because they had the same red marks on their behinds as I did. We were too young to understand it all; I was six, Khiem was five, and Mui was four. What we understood at that age was the consequences of our father's anger, what he was to us. In his eyes, we saw our father—the man who picked us up from Grandmother's house after school, the man who bathed us, cooked for us, and took care of us until our mother returned home from work. Until she returned from work. This was what we knew.

♦ ♦ ♦

We laugh about it now.

"Remember when Dad slapped you and you went"—she jerks her head abruptly to one side—"ugh!" Stephanie laughs.

"Shut up!" I say, grinning.

"I remember, it was in Chinatown and you cried." Khiem smiles.

"It was a long time ago," I say, swallowing their words down my throat. "A long time ago."

My Hmong Father

Kay Vu-Lee

You knew everything when I was young.
You tiptoed in to tie my shoe laces
and nudged me to wake during preschool naps.
You read foreign words from the Bible,
my memory verses.
I cried and told you I couldn't memorize them
because I couldn't speak English.
You took care of me.
Now, your hair is gray
and I
have to fill out your address change.

Where's the man who rebelled
against the Communists?
You were so strong;
you left your home and relatives to find freedom.
You were so courageous;
the close-by blast of grenades
did not stop you from carrying me
across the Mekong.
You were cunning
to get past
the Pathet Lao soldiers.
Thousands of men died trying, but you didn't.

After twenty-three years in America,
the land of the free,
the home of the brave,
you've become weak and scared,
trapped inside yourself,
this family,
this religion,
this ethnicity.

The Pilgrimage

Minh-Mai Hoang

In my family, faith had been an heirloom. We had a monsignor and several priests going back three generations. They lived in a region of northern Vietnam where the terrain buckled with religious fervor. My father had been a deacon in the parish of Phat Diem. That massive stone cathedral could rival any in Europe, so he said. Of course, my father had never been to Europe, but he had seen pictures. Chartres, Notre Dame, Canterbury, San Marco. Gilded rafters and stained glass. Trappings of a gaudy faith. We had the ardor—the mortar—of the humble, he said. That made Phat Diem a true and living house of God.

My father now found himself in Hayward, California. A long way from Phat Diem. He had a new life and a new place of worship. But he still spoke of his church, often over a thimble of bitter tea before we went to Mass at Church of the Holy Sepulcher. My father's voice softened when he spoke of his past. I'd like to think it was for my benefit, but perhaps he didn't want to wake my mother. She worked the night shift cleaning hospital floors and would not be up for hours.

I listened to his stories and tried to imagine a cathedral built out of huge, squat stones from Ninh Binh's quarries. The warren of chapels, each facing a cardinal direction. The statues of apostles seated in lotus positions. The chancel and trimmings expertly carved from local hardwoods. The eaves that curved mightily like trumpets.

We used to walk to church before the bells rang. Good thing I was with your grandfather because it was still dark outside. On days when the fog was thick, I could not even see the pond in front of the church until I almost stumbled into it. All I could make out was a white figure hovering just above the water, with its arms reaching out. Just like in the story my brother told me when we were under the covers at night. About a ghost who lured children near water so that they would drown. I knew it was just a statue, but, God forgive me, I wanted to turn and run.

"Dad," I asked in English, "didn't you know who it was?"

My father laughed.

The Lord Jesus Christ had been calling him to prayer.

After the tea, we walked to the brick church next door where I helped served Communion to about a dozen of the truly devout.

Mostly elderly people, and a few vagrants trying to get out of the cold. From my altar boy station I could easily see my father's movements during the service. He sat near the front, the "Daily Bread" prayerbook on his lap. When the appropriate time came, he would turn to the right page and run his finger along the Apostles' Creed, fumbling with the English words like the buttons of an ill-fitting coat as the congregation droned on.

I knew his mind wasn't always on the ritual. The Word was delivered in words he couldn't understand. For all his devotion, my father's attention often strayed. His eyes often went past Father Vincent to the alabaster Jesus splayed on a plain wooden cross. Sometimes he would train his eyes on a candle so intently I thought he had hypnotized himself. Most of the time, he sat there in the fourth row, looking sleepy but contented. I thought I saw a man grateful for his bounty—a modest life and the chance to start again.

Nightly, we thanked the Lord for our deliverance from death at sea, and communism. My father would lead the chanting of the rosary as the year-round Christmas lights flickered on the altar. His voice was like a metronome to which my mother and I kept time.

◆ ◆ ◆

My wife, Sara, and I were still on our honeymoon when my father passed away.

My mother didn't know how to reach us, so we didn't find out until I called ten days later from Rome. They went ahead and buried him without us. Apparently, he died of a heart attack while tending the graves at Holy Sepulcher. That had been his job for more than twenty years. My father never missed a day of work, and he worked six days a week, often on Sundays. He never left work because we lived on the premises. That was one of the perks of being caretaker, the free housing. My father liked his job, even though he turned down Father Vincent's offer at first. He didn't want us living in the small cottage on the cemetery grounds. Ghosts at our doorstep. Other people's ancestors. Mourners, vandals, cultists. Mostly, I think he dreaded the prospect of closing the gates and locking us in as night fell.

The gardeners said they found him lying in front of a stone cross, a wheelbarrow by his side. His legs had given way and he pitched forward, his chin punching the grass before the rest of his face. He had been weeding, something he hadn't done in years. My mother said she didn't know why he was weeding that day when he should have been making the schedule of graveside services with the local mortuaries. I think the poor man's knees had been bent in supplication when he felt the tightening in his chest.

When I try to recall what I had been doing at that very moment, I think I was probably riding a waterbus in Venice. For my own good, Sara dragged me to churches and museums to look at the art. That was her field of interest. Back home, Sara edited audio guide scripts for a San Francisco museum. Most of the time, I followed obediently as she explained Titian and chiaroscuro to me, often in a church.

I was probably at the Vatican when they buried him at Holy Sepulcher. I would be lying if I said I knew exactly what I was doing when they lowered him into the ground. My guess was that Sara and I had our heads tilted at unnatural angles looking at the ceiling of the Sistine Chapel. Still playing American tourists.

"Here, Tom, do you want these?" she said, handing me the binoculars.

"No, thanks, just the naked eye for me."

As I said, Sara was the art expert. I get drawn in mostly by the subject matter. In this case, it was almost every lesson I studied in Sunday school. Characters from the Bible come to life on a vaulted canvas. I could make out, even from the distance of several stories, the drunken Noah whose sons had to cover up his nakedness.

As I looked upon painted scenes from the lives of prophets, I felt a certain closeness to my father. Maybe even a gladness about the way he raised me. By that I mean Catholic. By that I mean privy to the Christian canon. Unlike the Japanese tourists around me, I didn't have to look up everything in a guidebook. There was St. Bartholomew holding his own flayed skin. There was the Pharaoh's wife rescuing baby Moses from the reeds. There were Jonas, Joel, Zacharias, Jeremiah.

This was my reward for years of catechism. Familiarity. Inclusion. Things that should have been strange to slanted eyes were made recognizable by reference and rote. Swords into plowshares. Water into wine. Lamb of God, you take away the sins of the world. I am the Light and the Life. Repent. Believe. Redeem. Forgive. I knew the lyrics to the anthem. I freely pledged my allegiance, my

Apostles' Creed. It was why I was able to adapt, to succeed in this nation under God. In the visible, with bitter tea and just us for all. It was something to believe in. Did it matter what? Huddled masses yearning to be free. Amber waves of grain, fruited plains. God bless America. Land of the free, home of the brave, play ball.

"Thomas?"

I uncrooked my head and turned to my wife. She looked worried.

"I'm fine, just having a conversation with the art. What do you always say? The art opened up its mouth and spoke to you in complete sentences?"

"If I didn't know better, I'd think you were making fun of me."

I turned my head skyward, silently thanking her for bringing me back to myself. I realized the shakiness of my insight, its desperation. Maybe what I was trying to do was rationalize my way back to my father. To forgive him by thanking him for something.

♦ ♦ ♦

The truth is, my father was an infidel of sorts. I had suspected as much when the letters began arriving soon after I started high school. Once in a while, among the mass mailers and bills, I came across an envelope with blue-and-red trim. It had foreign stamps, the Par Avion imprint, and handwriting with dots, hats, and slashes. The letters were posted from Sai Gon, then Bangkok, then Bolsa, California. There was never a name on the return address. With every letter, I could be sure the fighting would start that night. From the pullout couch in the living room where I slept, I could hear her volleys and his hiccups from the past.

To track us down!

—a nurse. I was recovering in Sai Gon.

People talking—

—wartime.

He doesn't look like you.

—the money!

To be perfectly honest, it didn't bother me that he had been unfaithful to my mother. He came into sainthood later in life. It bothered me more that he had sired another son. I suppose I should have been happy that I now had half of a brother. But my thoughts were small and starved. If I thought of the boy at all, it was with a child's wounded sense of justice. My father had been doling out his affections. His loyalties had been divided.

My parents never discussed the second family with me, and I probably would have left the matter alone but a little boy's voice wouldn't let that be.

I was stepping in the front door, basketball in hand, when the phone rang. I saw the wheelbarrow by the garage, so I knew my father was home that Friday afternoon. The phone rang twice, then it stopped. I figured the call was for me, so I picked up the extension in the kitchen. A son's voice asked for Ho Thai Son, and my father answered. I was not used to his phone voice, so reassuring and expert at tender phrases. I don't remember the words. Just a woman's voice asking many times—*When?*

I put the receiver down as quietly as possible.

The next morning, I didn't leap out of bed when the alarm rang at six. That had been my routine for as long as I could remember. Somehow my father had gotten the idea that he would lose his job if we didn't hear Mass every day at seven. He said the parishioners had all chipped in to sponsor a boatload of refugees.

These people took us in. They gave us a house to live in. I have a job and you study at the school for free. We have to show our gratitude to them and to God.

On that particular morning, however, going to church with my father felt disrespectful to God. I no longer believed, if that is the right word, that this man honored any commandments, even if they were writ in stone and slung about his neck. I pulled the donated blankets over my head, making a tent of warm air to keep sleep in. I heard him put the water on for tea. That would give me a few more minutes. Just as I dipped back into sleep, I felt cold hands on my ankles.

Wake up, son. Time to get up.

In my stupor, I thought I felt the touch of the risen dead. So many of them buried just outside our door. I knew they would come for me one day like they did in the movies. I kicked at this creature through the covers and woke with my legs tangled in blankets.

When the kettle sounded, I sat up and saw my father crumpled on the floor. Recognition at what I had done. Regret. Concern. An instant can only contain so much. There was no room left for a son's hurt and disapproval. It was probably the last time I ever looked at my father without being distracted by his lies. But for all my apologies, he stayed huddled on the ground. I was afraid I had seriously injured him until I heard him muttering his oaths. Prayers muffled by the shag carpet at my feet. The kettle continued to whistle until my mother appeared, weary-eyed, from the bedroom to remove it from the burner.

A few months later, I left for college back east. Years passed before we spoke again. My mother called twice a month to relay news. She told me about his failing health, I told her about my law school interviews. We kept up this arrangement even when I moved back to California to take a position with a San Francisco law firm.

Without ever speaking, my father and I came to an understanding that we would not talk of certain things. I took it as a sign of contrition that my father didn't oppose my marriage even though Sara was Jewish. He never asked me how we would raise our kids, and I never asked him about his other son. That was my way of covering up his nakedness.

◆   ◆   ◆

After my father died, Ma moved in with us. She still said the nightly prayers, but she did so quietly in her room in front of an altar she had set up on her dresser. There were two framed photos. One of Jesus with his sacred heart hovering over his chest. On either side of this photo were pillar candles with images of Our Lady of Lourdes set in red wax. The other photo was of my father. A black-and-white picture taken in Vietnam, soon after he left the seminary to become a soldier. His lips were sternly set and his eyes seemed to know of lost battles. But I guess you're supposed to see defeat in a photo of someone dead.

Sometimes when I walked by on my way to bed, I heard chanting. An unaccompanied voice. An old woman alone with her faith. On one of those nights, my mother opened her door as I lingered a beat too long.

Tonight is the second anniversary of your father's death, she said. Come pray with your mother.

Fingering the beads of my father's wooden rosary, I mumbled my way through the prayer cycle. As I had done as an altar boy, I stole a glance at my father. He must have been the age I am now. Already the creases around his mouth were showing signs of grim. I bowed to his memory. To the burden he must have carried in his heart. The one that pulled his knees to the damp grass on the day he died.

◆ ◆ ◆

"I think you're actually getting excited," Sara said as I strung the camera's strap through my belt loops.

My law firm, which advises foreign investors in Vietnam, had sent me to Hanoi to scout out the possibility of an office there. Even though I had my reservations about going back to a country I barely remembered, I couldn't pass up the chance to visit my father's old church. It was the compelling combination of curiosity, a vague sense of duty, and a nagging wife. Sara had been eager to visit Vietnam ever since we met at Georgetown. Her peacenik parents had protested the war, so she grew up hearing sympathetic stories about revolutionary peasants fighting against American imperialism. Sometimes I think she forgets my family fought for the wrong side. I couldn't resist reminding her that these days, V.C. doesn't stand for Viet Cong. It stands for venture capitalist.

Sara was right. I was getting excited about our day trip to Phat Diem, just a few hours south of Hanoi.

The drive to the cathedral was quite a buildup. Within ten miles of Phat Diem, churches appeared by the side of the road, about half a mile apart. They came in all kinds of styles. Sara recognized Gothic, Renaissance, Romanesque. Some were made of wood, others of brick or stone.

But I was disturbed by the way they stood out against a landscape of half-farmed hectares. Like the churches, the fields seemed abandoned. Probably because the ground was too hard or the weather was too clammy and cold. December was miserable in northern Vietnam. I could see no source of water nearby. It looked like the farmers had thrown down their plows in frustration and started sowing churches.

"This is unreal," my wife said. "It's like somebody just plopped them down here. Europe must be missing a few churches."

She began flipping through her guidebook.

"I tried to warn you. This is my father's turf. Catholic country," I said.

"Do you really think there are enough people for all these churches?"

It was a good question. There was hardly any traffic on the road, except for the occasional sputtering truck and a few motorscooters. Since the town of Ninh Binh, I noticed only a thin line of houses along the road and very few signs of settlement beyond it.

"These old churches must be left over from the French days," I said. "Before the Catholics went south to get away from Commies."

I glanced at the driver to check his reaction. Maybe he wouldn't appreciate the last bit—Vietnam was flirting with economic reforms but it was still a communist state. Luckily, the driver's eyes were on a coal truck he was dangerously trying to pass.

"What did they worship in before the French came along?" Sara said, not caring that two of the passengers were obviously French tourists. They had just been telling us about their trip to Dien Bien Phu.

Knowing Sara, she was probably wondering why the Vietnamese had traded in their gods. We had just come from a nearby set of ancestral shrines built by the Dinh emperors some centuries ago. They might have been interesting once, but now they were basically small crumbling houses sprinkled like weeds inside a modest courtyard. Only the Chinese-style eaves and faded calligraphy on the pillars alerted the tourist to their past uses.

Each shrine had an old woman attendant who sold you incense to light for a dead king if you wished. My wife dropped a ten thousand dong note, worth about a dollar, into the donation box and lit several sticks. She seemed to take the gesture seriously, entranced by the decay and oldness around her. Perhaps my earnest American wife believed she was experiencing something ethnic.

I felt a little embarrassed. For her, because her hunger for culture was so frank, but also for myself because my culture could only offer her pseudo-Sino relics of a vassal state. As she looked through her guidebook for mention of Phat Diem, I girded myself for what she would find. Once again under colonial might, the Vietnamese adopt, adapt—for some, their very faith.

So what if they switched faiths, I argued with myself. Taking on was not the same as giving in. Prayers or mantras. Bibles or sutras. Does it really matter? One system is as good as the next. You bend at the knee. You bow to circumstance.

"Must be a hoot around Christmas," I managed to say as we arrived. The Hanoitourist minivan pulled into a muddy parking lot reserved for Phat Diem's visitors. Some of them, our guide explained in serviceable English, were pilgrims who traveled from Catholic regions in the south. Dong Nai, mostly.

As we neared the church on foot, a company of trinket sellers quickly fell in line behind us.

"Madame, you buy. I give you good price," said a boy selling rosaries made of wooden beads. My wife smiled at him, pointed to me, then concentrated on wiping off the mud splatters on her khaki coatdress. We joked that it was my job to deal with the locals. I bargained hard with the boy in my patchy Vietnamese before buying a strand for my mother.

With vendors at our heels, Sara and I arrived at the pond where my father once saw Christ rising above the water. Instead of the green he spoke of, the water was now mud brown. The stone complex was certainly sprawling as my father described. But the stones were covered in mildew. Either Phat Diem had changed or my father's memory had failed him.

We walked across the wide courtyard and entered the church. I could feel the cold seeping into the folds of my jeans. It was like entering a grotto, dim and redolent of a wet earthy smell. The main source of light came from the open double doors. The weak glow from an overcast sky highlighted the rotting wood detail.

Sara clasped my hand and we walked toward the altar where my father once prayed. We sidled into a pew near the front, still holding hands. I thought of our European honeymoon two years earlier when I had set off in search of the fabled Notre Dame. Like a moron, I staggered in disappointment around the grounds of St. Severin for several minutes before I realized I had the wrong church.

◆ ◆ ◆

It was getting late and I had an early meeting with the Ministry of Planning and Investment the next day. I looked around for the tour guide. As I waited for Sara to buy more woven baskets, I saw a group of children getting ready to march into the church.

Each child wore a white shirt with a blue scarf tied around the neck. Sewn on the triangles hanging down their backs were yellow crosses. They must be the Eucharistic Youth League my father told me about. A young woman with a red scarf, probably the group leader, was making her way down the ranks, counting heads and straightening collars and neckties. Before she could get to the end of the line, a boy quickly shoved a net bag full of marbles into his pocket.

I don't know—perhaps I just don't remember—if I ever played marbles in the red, laterite dirt of Vietnam. But watching that boy, I could almost feel my forefinger poised over a clear bead with a yellow flame encased in it like a bug in amber. My finger straightened out in a flick, but it only hit the lining of my pocket.

I was too young when I left Vietnam to have any real, verifiable memories. But I read somewhere that there are memories you inherit. Emblematic ones that tell you who you are. That they just come upon you as you walk along ancestral paths. I must have covered every inch of flagstone at Phat Diem, and nothing descended upon me but a certainty that you can't conjure up an alternate past. That you hold no claim to something you never acknowledged, even if it was an heirloom.

"Tom, look up," Sara said. "Move over so I can get the church in the background. How perfect! Return of the Native! Okay, now give us a smile."

Ever since we landed at Noi Bai airport, she had been calling me Thomas Hardy, but now the joke was getting thin.

"That's a rather stingy grin. Come on, it's for your mother," she said. "Could we please unclench some muscles?"

"Sara, you've been running around like some crazed tourist all day," I said, knowing that I should stop right there. If I went any further down this path, it would be a very sullen and bumpy two-hour ride back to the hotel. But I was still annoyed at her for taking pictures of the altar even when the guide told her not to. "Don't you think you've used up enough film for one moldy old church?"

She snapped the picture and walked with quick strides toward the crypt of Phat Diem's founding priest. I knew she expected me to go to her and make amends. I could see her already heading back to the parking lot. In a few moments, she would be taking her seat on the bus, probably staring out the window as she replayed my words. By now, the other sightseers, the French couple and some Australian backpackers, had already piled on. They were all waiting for me. Soon I would be joining them for our ride away from here. But for now I stood rooted where I was, and watched the troop of boys and girls make their way into my father's church.

At 120 over 80

Aurora Harris

We see your cracked black gray
as mummified as Buddha's
sticking out from ultra
white bleached sheets.
Toes are gnarled and leaning
like a bundle of twigs wearing
dutch elm disease while the
straws in your nose sucking
florets of rose
appear to jerk air through sacs
above bleeding.

As a good Catholic girl,
I look for signs
and that river of saline
becomes one of them—
each drop is a bead
of the rosary in my pocket
that asks God to breathe life
into your Muslim foot . . .

It has trampled the earth
seventy-five of your years,
walked me through peat moss
and fields of white onions—
it's too young for my heaven
above your ripped spleen.

All I can do
is give you the words
that you'd want to hear:

Allahu akbar, Daddy.
Allahu akbar, Daddy

Daddy?
Maybe after healing
with chlorophyll and comfrey,
we'll jump like the Zulu
you once told me about.

Wedlock

Vince Gotera

Papa said, "You know I would have to kill you,"
to Mama, who sat quietly, head bowed.
I was just a kid—five or six—and cried
deep gut-wrenching sobs. The moon like a new
coin in the window, sliced in half by blue
knives of cloud. "You're too young to understand,
Vin," he smiled. "It would be my duty as a man."
A tear on her cheek, Mama whispered, "That's true."

To this day, I don't know if there was another man
or if they were only talking possibility,
in case, for example, Mama felt her face
begin to flush downstairs with a repairman.
Her only safety net then—Papa's motto,
A place for everything, everything in its place.

brother 2

Lan Duong

medallions
that he never
received
for fighting
the viet cong in '72,
brother 2's scars
lay
on his back
that is
mottled,
dusted with ash—
good camouflage
in the jungle,
he once told me.

but here,
the color of cork,
the color of yellow,
his scars are
round water-
marks
he cannot
blot,
pocked land-
marks
he cannot
return to.

on days
he is not cutting up
catfish and eel
or bagging
pork bones
on checkered floors
that are slick
with slime,
his lanky body sits
in front of the tv,
he is
smoking
marlboro
reds
laughing at jack
from 3's company
hand behind his back,
underneath his pajamas,
my brother fingers
the places
where
he has been.

Presentación Vega Gotico

M. G. Sorongon

She took up too much space, surprising
for such a small woman. The spare room
smelled halfway between baby powder
and death. I imagined the white cloud seeping
under my door at night. Each afternoon, trying
to thread needles at our sewing lessons,
I held my cautious breath, only inhaling
through the mouth. These things I remember:
Porcelana, margarine, roses made
from scraps of silk. Her husband, my Lolo, snarled
about the Japs still, and told stories of hiding
in foxholes. He kept a gun in the house,
amid my mother's protests: Pa, you can't
shoot people, not in Michigan. Lola kept
on sewing. They made her feel safe, the gun
and the sewing. I wanted store-bought dresses.
I wanted to call her Grandma, not Lola,
because my friends sang Barry Manilow
and laughed when she answered the phone. Her name
was Lola, she was a showgirl. She was
the prettiest of the six sisters, they said,
with the straightest nose, the fairest skin.
I saw only veins and bones, veins and bones
under half-live paper, and blue-silver hair curled
by a woman named Nancy, twice a month.
Michigan was too cold for her. She longed
for the heat, the mangoes, the dust kicked up
by the jeepneys. I was only twelve that December
when she faded away from us like some gothic star,
away from us and the silent, stoic cornfields,
and I did not know then what I know now:
that I, too, would come to long for the heat,
would stare at my veins and wish for hers,
would pick up a bit of fabric and try
to roll it into a lasting bloom.

Reincarnate

LeAna B. Gloor

My dead grandfather has become this old Filipino man
who walks by my house every day shuffling along
the broken sidewalk, always looking down.
I recognize his posture, the stooped shoulders, wide face,
the forever dyed-black hair on an eighty-year-old head.

I don't try to talk to him because I don't speak his language
and never did. Even when he stuffed wadded up dollar bills
into my fingers, muttering half English words about food and
haircuts, I never understood him.
And now, as I see him every day, this pitiable creature
walking back and forth in front of my house,
he is even more foreign, and I am even more afraid.
This new old man that he has become doesn't offer me money
or apologies, and I don't trust him.
When I see him walking by, I lock my door.

Uncle Died for His Country

Hanh Hoang

I hold his picture
of twenty years
embalmed
in mothballs.

My insides
quartered
like his face, a bomb splintered
splattered

or was it a howitzer, a rifle
Did it look like the wrinkled cow brain
my mother fed us?
or the gashed moon?

He grins.
Did he know he would die
soon

my uncle.
Not yet eighteen,
still the retarded look of youth

Zits.

Relations

Mayli Vang

Father left when I was five
he dwells among the dead
in a land foreign to my imagination.

Remnants of his existence:
A black-and-white wallet-size picture,
a faded yellow shirt.

Mother keeps to the living room
sewing her life into cloth
too fearful to confront the world.

She has sewn forty patches of:
Make New Friends and Keep the Old
as Silver, the New Ones Gold.

Sister inhabits the kitchen
cooking her dreams away
the perfect daughter.

Wednesday's menu for dinner:
rice, chicken boiled with bitter melon,
baby bok with garlic and pork.

Brother is nowhere to be found
out roaming the world he will inherit
he's a man, okay.

Friday afternoon: a police officer
escorts him home for stealing
a Nestlé crunch bar at J.J. Newberry's.

I am in my room where thoughts
are locked in books and dreams
are stored on shelves. I'm still young

I keep telling myself.

2:30 A.M.: I am still writing
mother hits me on the head with my journal
can you eat straight A's?

She wants to know.

Community

Spell

M. G. Sorongon

Ay, Trining, Vangie, remember that old house behind the ihaw-ihawan we bought together after the last husband finally left for good? The one near Ames Methodist, that church with the crazy priest who had legs like a pig and muttered about Jesus wanting to save our souls? But our souls were already damned, right, so instead we saved that house and moved into it like we were still in school, hoarding our money in a coffee can for the new sink, curtains, the dinette set, Frigidaire. Sears got all our money, we were such good customers there, running in with our monthly payments Fridays before they closed, just after the hospitals gave us our checks, no? And then out to Big Boy's on North Michigan for our celebration dinner, celebration for the weekend, for payday, for our house, for the Frigidaire with only three, two, one more payment to make. Vangie would always order that southern fried chicken, with the biscuit and gravy you could cut with the butter knife. For me, I like the Big Boy Burger with ranch sauce and tomato, fries and drink included for $4.99. We'd talk in the dialect about the other customers, the senior citizens in plaid polyester that came every night for the salad bar and the Young at Heart menu. And no one could understand us, and we'd shriek at Vangie's imitations of our waitress's plastic smile and her That be all?, and no one was there to tell us to laugh more quietly, laugh covering your mouth and soundlessly, if you have to laugh at all. So we shrieked and chewed with our mouths open and slurped our Coca-Colas all we wanted, our mothers turning over in their graves back in the province to see their daughters acting this way at forty. Those were good times, di ba?

Trining, so jokey, even after that good-for-nothing showed up at our crazy yellow house with me and Vangie on call at St. Joseph's so we couldn't protect you. He banged on the door with his work boots, open sesame, yeah, and Trining just opened the door, expecting the mailman or the girl from next door looking for her cat again. And what could Trining do but let him in, she can't even say no to the Avon lady, much less this hole-in-the-head that her mother liked so much, even though she never met him, just in Trining's letters home about how guapo and musculado he was, and the picture in front of city hall where he's wearing a suit for the first and last time. But mamas can't tell a suit is borrowed in a picture like that, huh?

Vangie, you, and I came home to find him at the kitchen table drinking all the San Miguel we had saved for the nurses' potluck, remember, and Trining standing there in the kitchen doorway with her hands behind her back. She tried to smile, but we knew better. There was the second batch of dilis roasting in the radar range, a bowl full of the dried salted fish heads next to him, each head not bigger than a thumbtack. "Nice Frigidaire you've got, 'sus María y Joséf, where the hell you get the money for this place," he said, sucking the salt off his fingers, as if Trining hadn't been the one supporting him with her overtime since he came home drunk with his last paycheck. Vangie chased him out of the house with a broom and me with the snow shovel and he called us brujas, all three bruja dykes, frigid as our icebox. Trining just sat on the porch steps laughing, laughing, until he drove off in his ugly Buick. Then me and Vangie turned around and realized she was crying. "Jesus," she said, when her voice stopped shuddering. "He can't even be sip-sip to me when he wants something. He's like that carpet cleaner woman that always calls even though she knows we don't got wall-to-wall yet." And we laughed though it wasn't funny, really, until we smelled the dilis in the oven burning and ran in to put out the fire. Remember?

We got the three last beers in the icebox and sat on the porch flicking the fish heads over the railing, counting isaw, duha, tatlo, apat, lima, naming them after our husbands, Jimmy Aurelio, Rogelio Avila, Rey Lazaro, until the last one sailed over the edge and landed in the spring mud.

Generations of Laundry

Ira Sukrungruang

Every Saturday morning, Mother emptied all the laundry baskets into an extralarge potato sack. She entered my room when the sun cast early morning shadows onto pale blue walls and moved lightly to the far corner where the laundry basket sat. Quickly and quietly, she emptied the basket without dropping one article of clothing.

Sometimes, perhaps unknown to Mother, I lay still and watched her, pretending to be asleep with half-open eyes. Mother was beautiful then. It was a different kind of beauty, purer, barely touched by time. She did not have sags under her green eyes, nor were the undersides of her arms hanging like dead flesh. Back then, she did not wear the thick wire rim glasses she wears now, nor were her smile lines confused as frowns. Her skin was smooth, and her movements were soft.

After Mother placed all my clothes into the laundry sack, she hefted it into her small but strong arms and carried it out the door. Before she left the room, she turned to me and smiled. I smiled back through the thick comforter that covered half my face.

The older I became, the longer I slept on Saturdays. Mother still came into my room, but I was never awake to witness the morning ritual. Still, every Saturday when I awoke to the clanging of pots and pans downstairs in the kitchen, my laundry basket was empty.

Mother did everyone's laundry on Saturday: mine, my auntie Sue's, who has lived with us since my birth, and my father's before the divorce. During winters and on gray, wet days, Mother dried all the clothes in the laundry room. On hangers and clothespins, the clothes hung together on a line extending from one end of the room to the other. Although our house came equipped with a dryer, Mother never used it. She said, "It like monster wid hot breath. Da hot breath is bad magic. Make da clothes shrink. Make a noise like a head in it. I think who head it is, you know?" Mother loved to watch horror movies, so the image of dead heads in the dryer didn't surprise me.

Laundry day always made Mother happy, especially hot, sunny summer days when she could hang the clothes outside. The family's clothes hung on two separate clotheslines that V-ed out from a fence post to two ten-foot poles twenty yards away. The two poles were the supports to my basketball net.

In the summer, the back door opened to an array of wet clothes. The clotheslines stretched over six steps leading down to the door, and, sometimes, if I was not careful, I would plaster myself against a bed sheet or two and come out on the top step Downy fresh. Behind the basketball net, Mother's flower garden blossomed into full bloom every first of June. Mother said they were Thai flowers; she had brought the seeds from Thailand. Queen Sirikit roses twined in and out of a white wooden fence. Their large, bright-yellow heads craned up at Mother while she watered them. Marigolds and varieties of dahlias sprouted up from the fertile ground in a palette of colors: yellows, oranges, reds, and violets. Mother was proud of her little garden. She watered it in between loads of laundry.

Since my birth and before, Mother carried on the laundry tradition without pause.

♦ ♦ ♦

During my three-week visit to Thailand when I was sixteen, I changed clothes every time I bathed, which was about five times a day. The laundry hamper was always filled to the brim. Mother collected it as she did on Saturdays in the States. But laundry day in Thailand was every day.

She carried our basket of clothes to the backyard of my aunt's home. There she sat and talked with her sisters while scrubbing the clothes in a soapy water barrel, a grove of coconut trees surrounding the yard. Sometimes I would join her in the backyard, not to do laundry, but to search for snakes with Pokey and Bo Bo, the housedogs. Sometimes I would sit under an umbrella, sipping Thai iced tea, savoring its sweet, creamy taste.

Mother and her sisters sat in a tight circle around the barrel and talked about old times. The soap bubbles frothed around their hands and arms. They rolled their pant legs above their calves so that water would not splash on them. If I wasn't searching for snakes, I listened in on their conversations.

The one I remember most was about Mother's old boyfriend. I never pictured Mother being with anybody but my father. After their

village," Aunt Ta said. "All the girls, including all of us, liked him. But he liked your mom."

"Most pretty," Aunt Jeem giggled.

"Really? Tell me more about him."

Mother said, "Nothing much to say. Teenage love, dat all."

"No, no, no. Not all at all," Aunt Jeem said.

Mother began scrubbing one side of a shirt against the other vigorously. White bubbles foamed between her hands with each hard scrub.

"Upone came over every day, and every day your mom walked with him to the lake. They sat and talked till nighttime. Then she came home with a big smile and floaty eyes."

"You mean Mom was swooned? My mom? Mom?"

"What you think, I never young?" Mother asked. "You think I mama forever?"

"Yeah."

"Nope. Your mom is like any other young girl. She has feelings like young girls, and strong feelings for a young boy, right, Pe Nit?" Mother replied, "Dat's right. I young before." She swung the shirt over a clothesline directly behind her.

"What did he look like?"

Aunt Ta began, "He had—"

"Brown eyes," Mother interjected. "Verly short black hair like new style now. Tom Cruise hair. Tom Cruise smile, too."

Aunt Ta continued, "Very skinny with round glasses. Glasses like old people wear. What are they called?"

"Bifocals?" I said. I moved closer to Mother and leaned against her. She placed her foamy hand on top of mine.

"Yes, bifocals."

Aunt Jume asked, "What bifocal?"

"Wen tah," Mother said.

"Oh yes. Round like moon," she giggled.

"Mom, what did you do at the lake?"

"Only talk. Upone verly smart boy. He study to be doctor." Mother rolled our already dry socks into little balls. She stuffed them in the corner of the hamper. "One time we talk about future life. We talk almost midnight. Da star and moon out over the lake. Verly pretty dat night." Mother looked away. She seemed to breathe in air from the past, letting it linger longer in her before exhaling.

Aunt Ta said, "Daddy did not like you staying out late. He waited for you, remember? He was so angry, but he never yelled, just said to come in earlier next time."

"Did you ever kiss him, Mom?"

"Why you ask dat?" Mother turned to me with urgent eyes. "Do not remember."

I glanced at Aunt Ta and the others. They said nothing, but their smiles answered my question.

◆ ◆ ◆

My father's clothes were piled near the bottom step in separate but neat mounds—dress shirts in one pile, pants in another, and underwear and sock balls near the front door. It was not the first time I found my father's clothes on the bottom step. Actually, it was the second time. The first was when I returned home from high school one afternoon and his clothes were scattered all about. My aunt informed me that my parents had the same argument again. She said Mother, in an angry frenzy, began throwing my father's clothes down the stairs. My father just left, saying very little, and drove to the "other house." Although it wasn't the first time his clothes weren't found folded in his drawers, it was, however, the first time his clothes did not make the Saturday morning wash.

I was fifteen then. As I walked through his clothes, I thought to myself, We're making progress. Not any progress toward reconciliation between my two arguing parents, but progress toward an end, an inevitable divorce that was meant to happen six years before. In the years in between, I was their delay.

When the fighting started, I used to cover my ears and stain pillowcases with tears. Like most nine-year-old boys stuck between two disenchanted parents, I blamed myself. I blamed myself for their voices jolting me out of sleep at night, for their harsh words spoken in hushed tones whenever I was near, for taking sides, and later, I blamed myself for not taking one. They stayed together because of me. Because one time I ran away from home at night in cutoff sweats and a thin T-shirt, making clouds with my breath as I ran down a dark street. They followed me in the family van, sitting next to one another, yelling at me to get in the car.

"Fuck you! Get the hell away from me!" I said.

My mother leaned over my father—the closest I remember her being to him in the past few years. She pointed her finger at me, screaming with a red face, "Git in now, you hear me? Git in now!" And then I saw my father's stern eyes pass over me before I turned into someone's yard, leaping over the wooden fence in bare feet.

I ran until my chest hurt. When I stopped running, I climbed into the hull of a rocket ship slide in an empty school playground and wished for the rocket to take me away to a better place. A place where my father didn't sleep with another woman. A place where my mother didn't hit my father so much. A place where I could be nine.

Then I fell asleep. And for a brief moment the rocket flew me to that place and brought me back home, and I found myself in my bed and not recalling how I had gotten there and never asking.

Years later their fights became part of my life, like a fly that didn't go away but kept buzzing around my ears. I wished for them to be apart. I wished for the divorce. Finding my father's clothes in piles at the bottom step Saturday morning led me one step closer in having my wish come true, one step leading to the last a month later. My father's clothes were packed in two dark suitcases; in his pants and shirts were buried framed pictures of the family and of Mother.

I helped him pack.

◆　◆　◆

It was six in the morning. The sun's gleam pierced through the white curtains, lighting the dust particles in the laundry room into specks of gold. Outside, Mother hung clothes on the line. I knocked on the backdoor window and smiled. She waved to me as I opened the door and entered into the hot air.

"Sawad dee, ja," Mother said.

"Good morning, Mom."

"Nice hot day. Good day to hang clothes." She hung her white nurse's uniforms one next to the other—corresponding pants to corresponding shirt. Behind hers were my aunt's.

"Did you finish washing, Mom?"

"No. Two load more. Many clothes today. You wear once and throw in hamper. Still have nice smell, but when you throw in hamper, it mix wit da smelly clothes, den smell like da smelly clothes."

"But I hate wearing clothes more than once. You know that. It makes me feel unclean." I shivered and made a face. "Do you need me to help hang?"

"Of course I do," she said. "Good boy today, huh?"

"Good boy every day, Mom."

After all the clothes had been hung, Mother sat on a stool and hummed a Thai song. It was a tune sung by Sutate, the Thai equivalent of Frank Sinatra, a Las Vegas–type lounge singer who charmed the ladies with his thick baritone voice and words of love. Sutate came to America once and sang at our church—his world tour covering all Thai Buddhist communities across the country. It was a fiasco of hoots and hollers, as sixty-year-old women climbed over one another simply to touch his hand. Watching him perform, I understood for the first time the power of music. The Beatles' long shaggy hair and thick English accents helped make them popular. With Elvis, it was the seductive sway of his hips. But Sutate was bald. And his hips stopped swaying when he turned twenty, thirty years ago. His words were his charm. His charismatic walk in a belly-shaped tuxedo was his allure. At the end of every concert, Sutate searched for a lucky middle-aged woman to serenade; he strolled in between tables and batted eyes with overdressed, shiny-faced women. Mother was lucky that day, and two years later, she was still envied by every Thai woman in the state of Illinois.

Midway through the song, Mother asked quite unexpectedly, "You still boyfriend wit Vewonica?"

Feeling uncomfortable, I cleared my throat. "Veronica and I are dating, Mom."

"You know Vewonica not Thai."

"Really? I hadn't noticed." I plopped on the ground; my legs spread in opposite directions.

Talking to Mother about relationships always made my cheeks turn red. Mother always said, "You have Thai blood from two good parent. Remember who you are. You not like dem." After the divorce, Mother said, "You have Thai blood from one good parent." The rest was the same.

Mother raised me to be Thai, and in the first eight years of my life, she never spoke a word of English to me. English was a forbidden language. She never knew how the other kids at school treated me, how they'd push me to the ground because I talked funny. Back then, the suburb I lived in was predominately white. We were the first non-Christian, nonwhite family to inhabit the south suburban neighborhood, fifteen minutes from Chicago.

One day, a group of sixth graders held me down while one of them punched my stomach. I was walking home from school. I was in second grade. No one stopped to help. When I arrived home, tears streaming down my face and grass stains on my shirt and pants, I vomited.

After that day, Mother integrated English into her Thai. She would say, "Ila, auk pi ting caya. Now, you hear me? Tamie watch TV?" And I'd respond in English without being reprimanded, "Mom, I'll take the garbage out later."

To Mother, a relationship with an "Amereecan woman" always ended in heartache. She would say, "Amereecan woman verly forward. Too sexy. Thai girl not like dat."

During my junior year in high school, I had a nervous breakdown in math class about a girl who broke my heart. She happened to be American, like the rest of the country.

After I whipped my books against the blackboard, Mr. Samenos, my math teacher, escorted me down to the school psychiatrist. He said: "Talk to the shrink, Ira. She can help you."

So I did, and like most psychiatrists, she said, "Tell me about your mother."

"Why is this important?" I asked.

"Do you talk to your mother about your feelings?"

"No."

"Well, I think you should."

I explained to the psychiatrist that Mother was from another country (sometimes I think from another world), and she would not understand. The psychiatrist insisted that Mother was no different from any other mother. "They all have experiences with life's ups and downs."

After an hour, I became tired of the whole thing, and said, "Okay, I'll talk to her," but I had no intention of doing that. When I arrived home, however, Mother waited by the door with pursed lips and crinkled eyes. I knew the shrink had called her.

I told her about the girl who broke my heart. She told me to find a Thai girlfriend. I told her I loved the girl. She told me there was no time for love, I should concentrate on school and go to college. After college, I could concentrate on love. General Mao of China concentrated on ruling a country, she said. I told her General Mao was a Communist. I was sent to my room.

Mother let the gentle breeze blow through her hair before she rubber-banded it into a ponytail. She looked at me and smiled. "No, Vewonica no Thai. You will marry Thai, yes? Thai girl verly pretty. I think you should call Kat. She verly pretty girl."

I shook my head and hid my face.

"She almost in high school. Only couple year difference," she said. "You are seventeen. She is fourteen. No difference at all."

"I just got my license and been in two accidents already. She's still hitching rides with her mom."

"No matter. She Thai. She pretty. She good cook." That was Mother's formula for the perfect wife.

My wife had to be beautiful so that I would not lose face when out in public. Men would look at my wife and say, "Lucky S.O.B., I wish I had me a wife like that." She would have long, lustrous black hair—hair that flowed down her back like a glistening moonlit river. And her eyes had to twinkle in the dark, so I would never lose her. And if I wrapped my arms around her, I could do it twice if it were possible, for she was slim but generous.

On top of that, she could cook.

When I was a baby, not yet able to walk, Mother said, I threw up Gerber banana mush and ate prechewed rice and fish sauce. Now, the thought of eating already chewed food makes me squirm, but I believe it was the beginning of my love for Thai food. I don't think I could live without having a spicy, sweet noodle dish, or a steamy bowl full of jasmine rice topped with a coconut milk soufflé. When I'm away from home for a long period of time, my stomach growls for Thai food, missing the combustion of flavors.

Being able to cook was one thing; being able to cook Thai food was another.

Mother and I sat and enjoyed the warm summer morning. A breeze swayed the clothes back and forth, spraying tiny drops of water on us like misty rain. After a comfortable silence, Mother rose from the stool and walked to the garage for a watering bucket. She filled it with water and added seven drops of liquid plant food.

"The flowers look beautiful," I said.

"Thank," Mother said. "You know, I have handsome boy, huh? A little big, but handsome. Uncle want you in movie in Thailand."

"Really? As what?"

"Hero, of course. My boy always hero."

I smiled.

"Do you like Vewonica?" Mother sprinkled the water on her flowers, looking intently at the ground, careful not to miss a spot.

"Yes," I replied.

"Be careful. Amereecan people divorce all da time."

"I thought I shouldn't worry about marriage till after college."

"Dat right, but don't want heart to be broken like last girl. What her name?"

"Jean."

"No more of dat, okay?"

I nodded.

The yellow roses seemed to glow more brilliantly in the sun after a good watering. A speck of water domed over the tip of a rose petal. The dahlias swayed to the rhythm of the wind, tilting to the right and nodding to the left like backup singers.

Mother lowered herself to the ground next to me. Periodically, she cocked her ears toward the back door, checking whether the second load was done.

"Friend call you yesterday, I think."

"You should take messages, Mom."

"Cannot keep up wid dem. Talk too fast like they are in hurry to go. I get tired. But girl call and I say you out wid Vewonica. Dat where you at, right?"

"No, but that's okay."

"So you were not out wid Vewonica?"

"No."

"Not having sex?"

I struggled to breathe. "Oh God."

"Oh Buddha."

"Oh God."

"What wrong wid you?" she asked.

56

"What made you say that?"

"I find a condom in wallet when I check da pockets of da pants before washing. Trojan. Why you have condom?" she asked.

I couldn't answer.

"Sex is not love. If find someone special, dan maybe, sex is dan love. But girls meet in bar, no, dat not love. Dat dangerous."

"I don't like bars," I said. "I can't even get in them."

"So you not having sex?"

"No, I'm not."

"Good. You old enough to think for yourself now. Responsible for own body and mind."

"I know."

Mother looked off into the horizon, miles away from where she sat. She closed her eyes and took a deep breath, her chest rising and sinking slowly. When she opened her eyes, she said, "I have a good son."

"The second load's done," I said, trying to breathe evenly again. Mother walked to the back door, avoiding all the hung clothes. I sat on the ground, twirling a piece of grass between my fingers. The sun shone down on me; its hot rays warmed my skin.

Mother hefted another laundry basket outside. Her back arched as she took one step at a time, always leading with the right leg. She plopped the basket onto the ground. I rose to help hang again. With little line left, we moved the clothes closer together so that the second load would fit. When the third load was finished, we waited until the hung clothes dried. Mother started humming again, picking up where she had left off in the Sutate tune that always made her smile.

Wrestling

Jon Pineda

Before the season, we were already pissed, our bodies tightening
                                                              around
ribs, our eyes, like panthers, sinking into shadows. We had given
                                                                  up

food, sweat until the air around us was heavy. The only thing we
                                                        cared about
was winning. At our first match, I wrestled a guy I had met
                                                      summers ago

at a Filipino gathering, a first communion or baptism. Down
by a man-made lake that separated the neighborhood in two, where

most of the children from the party had wandered, a few of the boys
pinned my shoulders against a tree while one punched me. I could
                                                                say

it was because I was only half, a mestizo, but that would be too
                                                        easy, I think.
We were just boys, happy in our anger. When they let me go, their
                                                        eyes clouded

as the lake, I didn't say a word. Years later, when I pulled
the one who had punched me down on the mat, I watched the clock

as I locked the breath inside his throat. He could have been my
                                                            brother,
his hair the same coarse black strands, his face filled with my
                                                            shadow.

I held him there in front of everyone.

Famine All Around

Sophie Nguyen

For all authors

They warn me and my family not to go to certain soup shops in Arlington, Virginia. These warnings come as anonymous notes left in our mailbox at night, strange phone calls that come at odd times, always catching us off guard. They are from the ones called the "overseas people."

"We better not see you at Pho Sixty-seven."

"We will hear about it if you go there."

"We are watching you."

"We assure you, something will happen to you and your family if you dare to eat there."

♦ ♦ ♦

It is because of the things I wrote in a book. They, the ones who watch, once admired me for things I wrote in that book. It helped their cause. So I don't go to the pho shops anymore, in Arlington, or anywhere else.

The shops are always crowded with large groups of people. Whole families gather in the mornings before the children go to school and the parents go to work. The atmosphere created by the noise of the people, the smell of nuoc mam and beef broth reminds us of when we ate in similar shops, before we all became the "overseas people."

At the more conventional lunch hour, the whites come in. The whites have discovered pho in recent years. They are just as addicted to it now as the others. Perhaps the smells jog some of their memories too, so they have become regulars at the pho shops. It's no wonder. A large bowl of pho can satisfy one's hunger all day, until dinnertime.

My family never knew who might be watching them when they ate, or who might be reading the things they wrote. That's why we've heeded the warnings.

Pho

- Defatted beef broth (northern style or leave the fat if you prefer the southern style)
- 2 star anise
- nuoc mam (fish sauce)
- 1 1/2 pieces of fresh ginger
- thinly sliced beef (London broil or other lean cut)
- 1 package of flat rice noodles (banh pho)
- cilantro
- basil
- hoisin sauce
- chopped green onion

Before these shops existed, I used to cook pho at home. It took two whole days to prepare when I made it the traditional way. Often, when I was writing, I forgot about everything else. I forgot about the fire under the soup and it boiled over, scorching the walls and ceiling of the kitchen. The apartment and its halls filled with a thick, oily smoke that offended the white neighbors. This was before they discovered pho and became addicted to it.

We suspect that the lease was not renewed because of the frequent fires. The pho was always better once it had been saved from the fire. The whites couldn't understand this. Despite the regularity of the fires, they always panicked, mistaking the art of cooking for chaos. Or perhaps, it was chaos and the process simply made room for it.

In the 1980s, pho shops began appearing all over the United States. My family frequented them because we were homesick, and we were just like everybody else except for the fact that I had written that book. Somehow, the words took the edge off the pain of being overseas and that made my family and me different. People recognized us and came to our table to talk. The owners of the pho shops gave me their business cards: my patronage was good for business.

Once, on a trip to visit relatives in the southern U.S., my family and I happened upon a pho shop called the Revolution. It was good for business, this name. The owner of the Revolution recognized me as the woman who wrote the book. He was an admirer of my work and we exchanged business cards. We ate and talked. I don't recall what was said; it was most likely small talk of some kind. When my family and I finished our meal, we left.

Eventually, I forgot about the restaurant, the soup, and the owner. Not that the soup was forgettable or bad; it was as good as any bowl of pho. The owner wasn't unusually friendly or remarkable in any way. He was just like all the rest who came to our table at restaurants.

It was purely by chance that we had come upon the place when we were hungry, and it satisfied our need so completely that it allowed me to forget.

It's the same with writing. It is difficult to say how it happens or if it really happens at all: writers forget things by writing them down. It's the readers who recall these things.

♦　♦　♦

After I wrote the history book, I continued my work in other ways. It was then that the death threats began to come, unaccompanied by business cards. The ones called "overseas" were now angry at me, so they wrote about me in their papers. I continued to work in spite of it, never repeating or referring to my family or to anyone else, the things that they wrote about me.

You see, my work took me back overseas to the place where revolutions happened regularly. You could almost say they happened consistently. It was this that angered the overseas people the most: that a woman should cross the line drawn by circumstances, a line that she had helped to define, and then, cross back.

It wasn't true that I was disloyal or forgetful of causes and lines. You could see it in my work, my actions and movements if you chose to: a loyalty of a different kind, which the "overseas people" chose not to see. For them, it was better to see the lines and to commit them to memory than to dare to look crosswise at history.

On that last trip, the cong-an paid me a visit at my hotel room on the morning after I arrived. I invited them in for tea.

"Stay as long as you like. Ask any questions. I will tell you anything you want to know."

"We have been reading about you in the Viet Kieu papers. We are very understanding people. We know you have your country's best interests in mind, so you will understand about the names."

It took a very long time to go through the list of names. I knew all of them and I carefully explained how I knew the person attached to each name . . . all except for one. It was just that one relationship, between name, place, and body, that I couldn't remember.

"Remember."

"I can't remember."

They waited for me to think of the name, to remember it for them, but I simply didn't know. So they helped me by reminding me that the name belonged to the owner of a pho shop.

"But there are so many pho shops that I've visited in my life and I've met the owners of most of them, if not all."

"The owner was very familiar with you. How could you forget someone who knows you so well and admires you so much?"

They waited and watched, reading my face. Again, they decided to help me remember. The restaurant was in the southern U.S. They know this because their people watch, always, everywhere we go and everything we do, even in the U.S., they can see.

They might have been on the verge of accusing me of withholding, but then, I did remember for them. "The shop was called the Revolution and it was in the southern U.S."

I explained that I had only eaten there once with my family, ". . . just by chance, because we happened upon it when we were hungry. The revolution had nothing to do with it. The owner had given me his business card, but I lost it. The owner called a few times, but I never returned any of the calls." It was just as I described before, about the soup, the names, and the forgetting. Except the part about the fire and chaos. We understood that in advance, so there was no need to discuss it.

There is a saying in that country. One uses it when one meets a friend who looks distraught or sad: "How come you look so down? You look as though you've lost your card!"

When I was a child, there was famine all around. Families were given ration cards for rice, and to lose one's card meant the whole family could go hungry for days. Some might not even survive. This is what I recall to myself when I work. The pain of an empty belly, the loss of a ration card, and the severe punishment that followed. We never forget the missing things: they become part of our bodies.

Keeping up with the Nguyens

Hanh Hoang

Everyone in the block thought the world of my family: my father worked as an engineer and our house was the best looking around. I, of course, was the most popular kid in the area.

Then the new neighbors came. I knew they meant trouble when they repainted their house turquoise and bought peonies and kumquat trees, a day after Mother painted our house blue and bought a few peonies.

"Turquoise!" Mother snorted, her lower lip protruded in scorn. "Such a garish color. Only bumpkins paint their houses turquoise." She laughed, but I knew she was upset; no one had outdone us before.

I, too, resented the new neighbors' thumbing their noses at us. Yes, it was obvious to me that was what they were trying to do, showing everyone they were better, that they had enough money to buy two more flower pots than we did.

I never saw the neighbors because our yard was separated from theirs by a high concrete wall. Still, their voices drifted over and I made out the family. There were three of them: the father, the older daughter, and the younger son, who whined often. The mother, it was rumored, had died recently, torn apart by a land mine in a village outside Saigon.

One day I became so curious that I climbed up on the roof of our house. I wanted to see what the neighbors looked like so that I could make fun of them later to other kids.

Peering down at the next-door garden, I saw a child of eleven or twelve, same age as me, playing alone. He squatted on the ground with only his pajama pants on. His right hand rhythmically threw a tennis ball up, grabbed some chopsticks, then caught the ball. As often as not he missed it. I knew the game well: it was for girls or boys much younger. With kids my age I played better games like insect fights, hide-and-seek, or mock judo battles. I wouldn't want others to see me with those chopsticks and call me a sissy.

And this kid talked to himself! When he grabbed the ball, he said, "Play so well, ha?" and laughed and threw his head back. When the ball fell, he said, "Should play better!" in a nasal high-pitched tone. Creepy.

I stood up and waved, but he didn't see. I broke off a piece of roof tile and threw it into his yard. He turned around and then went back to his sticks.

"Who is that?" he asked. "Don't know," he answered. Was he crazy because he had no mother or had he been born this way? This boy needed someone to talk to.

"*Psst.*" I could take him into my circle of fans. I could help him stage a cricket fight. Real easy. First you spit out some saliva, then you dip the crickets' heads into it to make them drunk, then you tie a strand of hair around their waist, twirl them, and there! They are ready for combat.

"*Psst.*"

He looked up. His face was flaccid, the skin translucent with a greenish tint like my mother's jade bracelet. Not a fighting boy, this neighbor. I rubbed the muscles of my forearms and felt sorry for him.

"Eh." I smiled, flailing and readying myself to jump from the roof, which was ten times my height above the ground. "Eh, watch."

The boy's eyes were wild with fear. His mouth opened and *prrrt!* this purple tongue lolled out. Spit flew. "Older Sister! come here." His voice quavered. "Old . . . Older Sister!"

Dumb. And now the sissy started to cry. It was just a fantasy, a make-believe. Did he think I was so stupid as to leap from here! I just wanted to make him laugh. Now he had to spoil everything. I scurried down the slope to the balcony because I didn't want any grown-up tattling that I climbed roofs. Mother had scolded me enough for making too much noise in the neighborhood. She was always afraid to lose face. "A gang leader," she had called me, rapping my head with her knuckles. "You are an engineer's son from a good family. Don't act as if you had no education!"

I was no gang leader. It wasn't my fault if all of us kids liked to sneak out in the afternoon when the grown-ups napped. Then, it was a world of our own with only us—me and Tung, Tuan, Hung, Dung, Bu—on the streets, no jitneys, no mopeds, no pedestrians, so peaceful! We gathered randomly, the group became bigger as we pranced in the tropical sun, everyone shoeless and shirtless with round, taut bellies showing. We decided on the spur of the moment on what we would play. I was usually the one to come up with ideas, but, honest, I didn't organize anything. The other kids followed me because they liked me. Sometimes when we were running down the main street, I suddenly turned into a blind alley, just like that, to test them, and sure enough, most of them trotted behind me, hollering, "Eh, he goes this way," to those who still straggled.

"Older Sister, come heeere." The next-door boy's voice broke, hysterical.

I skipped fast. I almost tripped on a tile. When I was at the end of the roof, I turned around before jumping onto our balcony.

The kid pulled himself up from the ground. He hobbled, his left foot dragging behind.

Poor boy. Not only was he dumb, he was a cripple.

For a long time I thought of the boy's legs and I felt sad. Whenever I saw beggars and cripples, I thought, what a pity, and sometimes I made myself cry—especially on rainy days. In my warm bed I imagined them huddling outside in the monsoon, helpless because they couldn't run as fast as the others and had nowhere to hide. I didn't cry over this boy, but I was curious. Why did he limp? Had he been with his mother when the mine blew up or did he have polio?

A few of my classmates had this disease and I always watched them walk without bending their knees, their hips lifted provocatively, their legs encased in a metal gear. They made me think of robots. I knew how robots walked because I had seen them in a Japanese movie. Sometimes robots and people with polio were one in my mind, so when my mother said that one day we would have only robots as servants, I imagined all these diseased people wobbling around in our kitchen. If I had this crippled boy as our servant, I would teach him how to be tough and not to whine. No one likes whiners.

◆ ◆ ◆

For months, passersby stopped in front of the house next door. "'*Sooo* pretty! And the flowers smell like lotus-seed desserts,' they say." Mother spoke in a mocking singsong voice as she took out from a lacquered box all the piastres she had saved. "I say the house is pretty like a monkey. I'll show them what pretty is."

Mother left with the wad of bills. When she came back several hours later, I could tell she was trying to hide her happiness because her nostrils flared a little and her lips were pinched. Behind her, two men carried a piano.

A piano!

In our neighborhood some families had mandolins, some had accordions, but no one had a piano. For three days the kids in our block came to watch the instrument. I gave them each a glass of water and explained to them how the little hammers inside created all the sounds. Even though several of the keys were broken and their white laminate yellowed (Mother had bought a secondhand piano), all the kids were impressed.

"Ma oi! This black box is big enough to sleep inside. Must be nice to sleep with all the strings *bing bing* around you."

"No. Feel it. It's nicer on top, it's so smooth and cool. Uiie! With a pillow and a glass of iced water for just before I fall asleep."

"No. More fun to cover it with a mosquito net and stay under. So cozy, like a little house."

But soon I started to hate the instrument because every morning Mother woke us up at five to make us practice. "Son!" She usually wiggled my big toes first then tickled my armpits, hoping that I would get up laughing and happy, but I refused to budge. I tensed up my toes instead. Finally she slapped me in the stomach, a little harder each time.

Toes, armpits, stomach—my God, what next? I sat up before she came up with another part of my body to torture. Five in the morning! This piano business had gone too far. How naive we kids were for thinking that the piano would bring better sleep.

"Son, play well, so people won't laugh at you."

"Ma, what have you done so people won't laugh at you?" I asked one day. Mother scowled. I rushed to the piano stool and started striking the keys. I could push Mother so far. I didn't want her to scold me all day, going on and on about how she sacrificed her life for us and for what, and her eyelids would droop, a little swollen, as if she were going to cry. Then, she looked both sad and mean and I would feel love and disgust for her.

My music sounded like banging from a body shop. "Are you happy now?" I finally asked.

"Not good enough, Son. Practice more, and it will come as easy as breaking wind."

I hated it! And I hated the music instructor, who had the face of a lion, bulging eyes and a snarling mouth. She didn't do anything to me, but she was mean to my older sister, even called her a decomposed buffalo. Buffalo are stupid, the instructor said, but when dead and decomposed, they are even more stupid.

Watching my sister listen quietly to the teacher, and quietly start again, just broke my heart, but Mother wouldn't listen when I told her. Sometimes I was so hurt I spent two hours sitting on the roof.

My sister, she just laughed it off. Every time I sat on top of the house listening to her play Schubert's sonatas and Bach's fugues, I understood why she was forgiving. Her notes drifted, sometimes dancing, sometimes sighing, oh, so beautiful that I could understand then what each composer tried to express in each piece.

I knew the new neighbors must be impressed with her music, too, because soon afterward they bought a piano.

♦ ♦ ♦

"Ma, I saw it. It's shiny and the keys are white, not orange like ours. It's big, Ma." I extended my arms to show how big it was.

"Those monkeys will just put it in their living room for decoration. Really a waste! They think anyone can play, but they won't know how to."

"Why not? They will take lessons like us. You said it's as easy as the wind." I spoke in her lecturing voice, pursed my lips, then snickered. I didn't like her to say one thing one day and another the next. Lying, that was what it was.

Mother pinched my buttocks, but I fled before she could do me further harm.

Later, I was proved right. The neighbors started to play—or rather, the older sister did, because how could the boy, crippled and all? But Mother wasn't too far off either, because these people really were monkeys. They imitated us, playing all the songs that my sister and I had played, first the easy ones, "Clair de Lune," "Frère Jacques," then as the months went by, classical music, "Danses villageoises," even Bach's "Imagination." They played awfully, the notes jumbled as if their fingers were too weak and short to strike the right keys, and strike them sharp, so confused. And there was no rhythm. Each song was a multitude of songs, unrecognizable, fast and slow and slow and fast, the mistakes so many there was no relief.

My head ached. I was tense and my heart always braced for the divorce, Mother shut herself off from the outside world. She seldom went out, even to church. She spent most of her time sitting by the living room window overlooking the neighborhood. Her sewing machine rested on a wooden table next to the window. She sewed every day.

When my aunts saw me creep over to listen, they invited me to join their circle. "Come sit here. We have much story to tell you about you mom."

"What stories?" I asked, folding up my pant legs.

"You mom pretty girl long time ago," my aunt Jume said.

"Not pretty anymore?" Mother asked.

"Too old to be pretty," Aunt Ta said. Out of all my aunts, Aunt Ta spoke English clearly with an accent more German than Thai; she had lived in Germany for twenty years.

"We are all too old to be pretty," my aunt continued. "But back then, your mama was the prettiest girl in the village. She had handsome guys like you knocking on her door every day. Sometimes they come three or four at a time with flowers in their hands like trained monkeys."

"Go, Mom," I said. Mother shook her head and smiled. "Did she go on dates?"

"What date?" Aunt Jeem asked. The skin between her eyes furrowed together, and she tilted her head to the side like a confused puppy.

"Auk pi teuw doy gan," Aunt Ta explained.

"Ahhhh . . . den she all da time on date."

"But your grandpa did not like it," said Aunt Ta. "The oldest daughter was supposed to take care of the family, but she goes and has fun with the boys all the time."

Mother smiled. She was not wearing her dentures and all her back teeth were missing. "I take care best I can. You all bad. Run and fight all da time."

"Did my mom have a boyfriend?"

My aunts whispered to one another in low-tone Thai. I barely understood the words, and even then I was not sure what they meant. Mother leaned back on her arms and looked into the sky. She waggled her feet back and forth, waiting for an answer as I did.

"We remember one boy. His name, I think, was Upone. Right, Pe Nit?" Mother nodded her head. "He was the handsomest boy in wrong notes. I now refused to practice. Why, people in the whole neighborhood were laughing at us now. They thought it was my sister and I who produced such a din because there was no telling who played what anymore.

I was mad that the new neighbors wanted us so to lose face, that they mocked and provoked us.

I made fun of the crippled boy with other kids. I limped, lolling my head as if I had no neck muscle, and talked to myself. "Play not good, ha? Should play better, ha?"

But even as I was clowning, I felt a little ashamed, the same shame as that time I tied firecrackers to a dog's tail. I was afraid the other kids thought badly of me.

I looked them in the eyes.

"His mother!" said Bu, my closest friend. He always said "his mother" when he was excited. "Is the boy really like that? How disgusting." Bu, too, started limping and rolling his head.

The other kids laughed. They wanted more.

◆ ◆ ◆

My sister didn't give a frog about the whole situation.

"Why are you still doing this?" I asked and rested my head on the piano; my eyes followed my sister's hands back and forth across the keyboard. "They will practice the same song next week, they will make people believe that you can't play."

"Let them." She flipped the music sheet and continued, her fingers fluttery like sparrows in flight. She knitted her brows in concentration, cross-eyed, looking so peaceful. She was pretty! I had never seen a nicer nose, small and upturned and so shiny it reflected the light.

"Why practice if it doesn't bring you honor?"

"Because I like to."

"Why? Teacher scolds you all the time."

"Let her."

Strange. I liked to eat, I liked to play games, but I never liked to do anything that required work. Work was duty, Mother taught us. Work was boring.

I banged the keyboard with my two fists and ran off. She doesn't care about honor, but I do. She will see. I will avenge the family. I don't know how, but I will.

But I couldn't help admiring Sister.

♦ ♦ ♦

The neighbors varied their repertoire now. All day long they played our songs and then several strange ones. The latter were loud, not like a crescendo, but unrelieved *boomboomboom,* with lots of fingers used. Mother said they were hymns.

"Music for Protestants," she said. "They are not even Catholics. The father works for Americans, so the monkeys want to prop the Americans' butts up by imitating them and becoming Protestants. In this religion, priests are allowed to marry and have children. Really perverted!"

Now, I didn't always agree with what my mother said, but this time I thought she was right. Bonzes and priests had never gotten married. Of course there were men who joined the monasteries to dodge the draft, and you could always tell who they were because they smoked and went to the cinema, and dirty goats that they were, they ogled women. Whenever I saw them, I yelled to their faces, "Fake bonzes! Fake priests!" But even these draft dodgers wouldn't dare get married.

The new neighbors, however, didn't care a whit about tradition. Every Sunday morning they played hymns and invited their friends over, and when the day ended, the next-door girl said, "I'm inviting you to come back next week," her overly feminine voice drifting to our side of the fence.

I climbed up the roof one Sunday for some new mischief. What could I do to shame this girl?

I started when I saw her. Heaven and earth, she looked ridiculous! A pink bouffant miniskirt and bouffant hairdo! And standing there with a group of young men, she shook her head in shy little jerks while giggling into her right hand.

"You're really talented," a man said and the others nodded. She blushed. When she talked to the best-looking men, those with square shoulders and thin waists, her face turned crimson. The men and I watched her and knew her longing.

69

I thought of my sister. Mother did not allow her to be with male friends and Sister would not dare invite them to come sing in our home.

"If you are from a good family like ours, people will hear about it," Mother said. "Men will flock to your parents to ask for your hand. No need to socialize with them. A waste of time."

Sister would have liked these men. They were handsome and they brimmed with intelligence, the kind of men who managed to have the draft deferred to pursue higher education. Sister, so pretty, wouldn't have the opportunities that this girl, so ugly, had.

And this girl wouldn't have been so ugly had it not been for her big bulbous nose, which wouldn't have been so ugly had it not been for the blackheads, so numerous and dark they made me think of strawberries.

"Hey, Miss, do something about your nose!" I was surprised even as the words escaped my mouth. Quickly I crawled to the other side, hidden from the view of the gable roof, and crouched, my head tucked to my chest. My heart thumped *thud, thud,* but no one would see me here. Perhaps those people, hearing a voice from above and not seeing anyone, would think it had been the voice of God, that he had responded to all their enthusiastic hymn belting.

Laughter bubbled in my throat.

Was I being mean? I thought for a moment and decided that no, I was doing her a service. Really, she should do something. My sister steamed her face every Friday night and squeezed all the blackheads out. She squeezed mine, too. "If you don't want your face disfigured for life, you should get rid of them," she said. It hurt and a yellow thin column rose with the blackhead on top, but that was it. Easy.

I continued laughing. I tried so hard to be quiet that my stomach hurt. When I lifted my head, I saw all of them—the boy, his sister, the guests—staring.

The girl's face was dark with rage and pain. No man would be interested in her now. When they looked at her, they could only see her nose.

♦ ♦ ♦

The neighbors bought a television.

Every evening at eight they opened their front door wide and people in the neighborhood came to the front yard to watch.

"Everyone's favorite program is the flower queen contest," Bu reported, noisily sucking on a sweet-and-tart tamarind candy I had given him. "It's to choose the most beautiful woman. All this flesh, his mother! The women walk on a platform in bathing suits looking really shy. 'Elephant thighs,' 'Idiotic smile,' or 'Younger Sister, put your clothes back on because your thighs ooze with lard,' people shout at the screen. These women deserve it, right? They shouldn't parade in a bathing suit for all to see like that." Bu looked embarrassed for a moment. "But I'm just telling you what the other kids told me. I have never gone to that crippled boy's house, so I didn't see the program myself, but Tung, Tuan, Hung, Dung, they all go there every day."

I knew Bu was telling the truth—that the other kids had switched sides—because they didn't come to play with me in the afternoons anymore. It was no fun for the two of us, Bu and me, to make noise in the streets, so instead I taught Bu some judo moves. After some halfhearted attempts at judo fights, we would go back to my house and I would make him a drink of condensed milk and ice cubes, lots of ice cubes because Bu loved them and his family didn't have a refrigerator.

Then the American series came. I could tell they were American because people on television spoke American and I could hear them even from my house, their language full of liquid sounds, with *r*'s, *i*'s, *w*'s, like water flowing on rocks. The series appeared in the evenings. I couldn't help being curious, so I climbed on a chair and watched over the fence. There were *Gunsmoke*, *Star Trek*, *Bonanza*, but it was *Mission Impossible* that Bu fell for. I didn't see him, but I heard him all right. Every time the good guys were getting caught, he shrieked, "His mother! His mother!"

Bu stopped coming to my house. I had nothing to do during nap time now. I sat every day on the roof to watch my former friends watch television, or when the set wasn't on, play ball and chopsticks with the cripple. Even Bu.

"You, your turn," the crippled boy would order, pointing at Bu. I was sure the boy talked with such arrogance to Bu because he knew Bu had been my best friend.

Bu squatted as the boy told him to, and awkwardly threw the ball and picked up the chopsticks. He always dropped some chopsticks, though, and the crippled boy would laugh so hard, and as he laughed he swallowed air and choked sometimes, the idiot, and my former friends laughed with him. Bu, shyly, laughed, too, while refusing to look up at the roof, where he knew I was. I couldn't help feeling embarrassed for him. He had lost all his pride, and now, crouching there, he was so humiliated that he dared not even blow his nose. Even from the roof I could see snot peeking out from his nostrils like two slow green caterpillars. I wanted to plead with the others, "Can't you see he's crying inside? Can't you see the snot is his tears?" But what for? They would have no pity.

I had no one to turn to, not even Mother or Sister. Mother, too, gave up now. She stopped talking about the neighbors and made believe she hadn't noticed that people in the block no longer found time to bow to her and greet her, "Salute to you, Mrs. Engineer."

And Sister, who had always been so sure of herself, asked me every day about the next-door girl, "What does she wear? She can't be as ugly as you say if all these boys keep coming." I told her to go climb the roof to see for herself, but she wouldn't. Too proud. We were a proud family. Yet, she constantly looked at herself in the mirror these days. She must have wondered why no man had heard of our family's good reputation and come to ask for her hand.

I had no heart to tell her not to hope too much. Since that day I had seen Bu at the neighbors', I had started talking, well, to myself. No, I wasn't crazy, just lonely. Very lonely.

Eating

My War with Slugs

Soul Choj Vang

Sunshine, my one-year-old daughter,
ate a slug one day. I only found out
when she hit her chin on the window sill,
bit her lower lip, and began to cry in shock
as she spewed blood, curdled milk, food, and
a piece of strange-looking
material onto my shirt.
I rubbed the thing between my fingers
and felt the slimy skin. When I squeezed,
out came its sticky intestines.

Since then I have been on a personal crusade
against those creatures of the dark
and damp crevices of the earth.
I flood their homes in the flowerbeds
in the front yard and sprinkle salt
on them when they climb up the wall or onto rocks.
They turn an amber color and begin to foam
in their death spasms.

When the salts can't keep up
with their numbers, I spray them
with foamy wheel cleaners. The smell
swarms through the house.
My wife complains bitterly. I don't listen;
I keep spraying, watching slugs freeze and die.

I think I have won the war;
it's been a while since I have seen any slugs.
Little do I know that they have gone
underground in preparation for a full-scale assault.
Lately, they have been creeping en masse
from under the walls into the spare room
that I had planned to be the babies' room.

They seem to anticipate me.
They must have spies somewhere
maybe inside me. Who knows, I could have
eaten a slug when I was a baby. And now it's there,
living near my heart, conspiring.

Floating Eden

Ruth Pe Palileo

When the Japanese bombed
American ships
the supplies
and the dead bodies
floated in the seas
surrounding the Philippines.

My father
and his friends
would swim out to
the cans of Spam
and the Hershey bars
and bring them back
to sandy shores.

These
tanned
skinny Asian boys
would hoard the corned beef hash
in secret places
in the woods
where they hid
from guerrillas.

"This," says my father,
"was how we developed a taste for America."

Legacy

Jora Trang

Today is a special day.
No skipping rooftops or
climbing trash bins today.
No tearing through the electrical attics
of this village, Little Saigon, today.

Today I will walk along the street
careful not to step on wayward cracks.
Today I will play my part, the escort,
as smaller children bump against me,
weaving in and out of foot traffic
lost in games I should be playing.

Savory smells of spice and sweet
slip trip from the shops within,
ducks red and marinated hung upside down,
touching and tasting things they sell,
with my grandmother at my side
in culture and colors, our distance hides.

She on the right, me on the left—
side by side, arm in arm, I hold
this legacy with no connection.
Words tongue tied in my mouth
twisting unfamiliar Vietnamese words
to break the ancient silence.

Through touch and smell, we communicate
I watch her hands touch everything—
fresh bread in the pastry shop,
round heads of children as they pass,
gentle silk of the ao dai,

but she never touches me.

Arm in arm,
connected by only an elbow pit,
her head shakes in age
mine in confusion.
I can't find the questions
the words, the wonderment.

Like this I walk—at her side,
I play my part, the escort,

but she never sees me.

I am the eldest of three,
the second in command,
but I am still the child

of my mother
a peasant woman—
her son's mistake.

And so, she never touches me.

Today is a special day.
Today she seeks the fruits of life
fresh sweet bright juicy oranges,
as if some secret jewel in storage,
she knows the seasons by heart.

With expert eyes she picks and chooses
touches life with aged hands
hands that have known distant pain.
Squeezes, smells, turns round and round
oranges both large and small
oranges of a sweet new scent.

Musk of age chiseled life
in the hands of life itself—
my grandmother minces past and present
years of sipping orange juice
years of growing orange trees
oranges across distant lands.

Then in twenty bright orange fruit
after twenty long chosen minutes
we walk once again, arm in arm,
without twenty fruits of life
away from the clamor of kids
the loud chatter of the people.

And I sit across the table
listening to the silent stories of past lives
unspoken advice my grandmother gives
as she peels this fruit of life,
gently stripping life barren
showing life in all its soul.

Wedges of sweet orange juice—
slips a piece through knowing lips
thoughtful, thinking, tasting, eating
this sweet orange, fruit of her life.
She scrunches her tired face
turns to look through my soul—

Again, she never sees me.

Whispers words I long to hold
in a world in which I held no power
finally we touch, communicate
seal the connection between the silence
I wait for the words
I wait for her touch . . .

"Take these oranges, they're too sour."

Chilies and Dried Anchovies

Shirley Geok-lin Lim

I never learned to cook the way young *Peranakan* women were supposed to do. If my life had been like my mother's, she would have taken me in hand when I turned six or seven and trained me to plant, pick, grind, mix, and simmer the many pinches and handfuls of spices and roots that make up *Nonya* cooking. But my life was to be nothing like my mother's. In fact, her later life was unrecognizable from the domestic role she had been trained for, for at about the age of thirty she gave up motherhood and left her unemployed husband and six children in a small town to work in a series of low-paying jobs in Singapore City, about two hundred miles away.

Peranakans, or assimilated Chinese who had lived in the British colony of Malacca for generations, were a gregarious, intimate community. But losing face, *tak muka,* the loss of the appearance of social respectability, was so traumatizing for them that families were crowded with unsociable skeletons: feebleminded children, womanizing husbands, illegitimate babies, abandoned wives, business failures. Perhaps *Peranakan* families did not have more of these than other communities. The secrecy and silence that breathed delicious gossip around these scandals permeated my early consciousness of my mother's people, rather like the mouthwatering fragrances of *lemak* (coconut-based sauces) and *pandan* (screw pine leaves, used for perfuming special dishes) that distinguished my favorite childhood breakfast of rice and *sambal.*

In my mother's life in Malacca, *Nonyas* carried their reputation for fine cooking like service medals. As *her* little girl, surrounded by her aunts and sisters and friends, it was borne upon me in both spoken and unspoken ways that cooking well was a woman's pride. When Mother still lived with us, when I was just five and six and seven, I remembered visits to and fro between our family and her relatives. Grand-Auntie lived a long way off, across the town center of Chinese shops and beside a Malay kampong of wooden houses raised on stilts. Her house appeared to lean into blue-pea-flowered hedges where we gathered the *bunga telang* for spotting her delicate *kuih kuih,* cakes rich with palm sugar, bananas, and coconuts, a startling violet color. Listening to the women's incomprehensible chatter, my wandering ear could understand only the elaborate compliments they paid each other on food preparation.

Nonya dishes are a scented herbal delight of numerous leaves, flowers, roots, fruit, spices, nuts, and chilies pounded together and slowly simmered with coconut or tamarind paste. No curry or *sambal* was ever the same, for the fresh ingredients were always subtly different. The lemon grass may be sharper on this occasion, the shallots more watery, the ginger younger and milder. Or the coconut may be maturer and more robust, the fermented prawn paste or *blachan* particularly pungent. For *Nonyas,* the complex smells of different herbs and spices are as important to food as its vivid appearance and ineffable taste. No one cooked with dried powders, packaged spices, bottled lemon juice, canned beans or factory-prepared sauces. Delicious food was a fundamental principle to the *Nonyas* and *Babas,* my mother's people, so central that their religion revolved around feeding their dead: fragrant bowls of ginger-soy pork, platters of gently steamed chickens, their pale-golden skins glistening with melted fat, placed on the altar table before the ancestral tablets and black-and-white portraits.

Mother was a sometime good cook. Most days the kitchen was ruled by a Chinese servant who had a free hand in shopping and preparing the dishes. But on special days like New Year's Eve or *Cheng Beng,* the day for commemorating the dead, Mother took over the kitchen and set to grinding, roasting, mixing, and stirring. The meals then were memorable, and completely of Mother's people, evolved from generations of Chinese-Malay contact: dark brews of chicken transformed by the earthy decay of candlenuts; large briny prawns, their long whiskers and sharp-shelled heads still bright in a turmeric pineapple broth.

Being a good cook did not bring Mother any luck or happiness. Her cooking, I figured very early in life, was a complicated social phenomenon that was both appreciated and not much good. Mother's life was an aberration. Whether the aberration was this early self, brilliant in the kitchen, or the older woman, living out the mediocre consequences of a separate independence, I still cannot tell. Her midlife change, from a traditional mother to an independent woman, proved that she rejected the values of domesticity. Great food is one thing, but it is not enough for a modern woman to be only a good cook. A modern working woman has neither time nor patience for the slow, arduous chopping, grinding, and simmering that *Nonya* cooking requires. Besides, living by herself in Singapore City, among its noted plethora of food stalls serving an amazing variety of Asian fast foods—Hokkien, Malay, Indonesian, Punjabi, Cantonese, Hainanese, South Indian—Mother never had cause again to labor on those elaborate dishes her mother had carefully taught her. Preadolescent and the only girl in her family of six children, I not only never learned to cook from Mother; I learned to despise the traditional fuss made over *Nonya* cooking as an outmoded social manner, hypocritical and somewhat sinister, the way I thought Mother's relatives were hypocritical and wicked after she left us, took refuge with them, and we were disowned by Grand-Auntie, aunties, cousins and all.

◆　◆　◆

Second Mother was also noted as a good cook, but because we were now so poor, her food was plain and cheap. She came into our family a year after Mother left. In that year I had so little to eat that, in a photograph of me taken at a class gathering, my elbows stuck out like twigs. Hunger was distressing. It hurt, made me tired, light-headed, and irritable. It was also shameful. I could not confess I was hungry the way I could say I had a fever or a stomachache. When I walked into a classmate's house after school, the smell of hot oil and frying shallots was like a fantasy, a luxury so out of reach I could enjoy it perfectly for its smell. How could a family afford to feed its dog a bowl of rice and meat, I wondered, when in our house there was not a speck of food, nothing left over, nothing stored, not even uncooked rice?

For some months, dinner was our only meal, and what joy we had in feasting on the rice and soup and small meat dish that Eldest Brother bought and carried home from the Central Market stall at 6 p.m.! No wonder Father, left with six hungry children and paid erratically by the clients he managed to find for the day, beamed at dinnertime. Every evening meal must have appeared as an achievement to him, the food produced in the brink of time, with the few dollars earned that day. He was a hand-to-mouth provider. There was never excess food. One moment rice and meat appeared on the table; in five minutes we had eaten it all and had to wait twenty-four hours for the next meal.

Second Mother's cooking brought a wonderful stability to Father's life, and an end to our hunger. Even with Father's uncertain earnings, we now had plenty of fresh steaming white rice, as much as my brothers could gobble down, served with *kiam chye*, salted cabbage soup: lots of soup, its flavor intensified by *ajinomoto,* monosodium glutamate crystals. Second Mother was hard pressed to feed us all, the children Mother had left behind in Malacca, Second Mother's own sons, and Father, still a finicky diner despite his run of bad luck and working-class petitioners who could pay only a few dollars for an entire day of paperwork. Besides, Second Mother was saving to buy a house someday. When Father ate dinner at home, we could look forward to mackerel, fried so well that their eyes popped out in a white jelly, as well as black soy fatty pork. But for lunch during school holidays, without Father, we had rice porridge, salted fish, and pickled cucumbers.

Food, like time, was a matter of survival in Second Mother's house. She was too busy scrubbing our clothes on the washboard, sewing dozens of trousers for the boys, or nursing the newest baby, to grind and mix the roots and spices that Mother did. She cooked like a South Chinese peasant, suspicious of spices and chilies, and thrifty with meat. Salt and *ajinomoto* were her main flavoring. She fed us bean sprouts, bittergourd, and kangkung, water convolvulus, huge damp clumps bought for ten to twenty cents from the vegetable peddler.

Second Mother never taught me to cook. At least, she never asked me to help in the kitchen. Perhaps it was because the kitchen, an open-air enclosure next to the concrete tank of water, was a tiny space, just a *dapor* or clay stand in which she set kindling wood ablaze. Squatting by the open drain, she prepared the vegetables with a quick, fierce energy, shaking the washed leaves and shredding them into bite-sized pieces. The salted fish, the stir-fried sprouts were on the table within a few minutes, together with the rice that had been steaming earlier. I did not think of her cooking as mysterious; rather, it appeared efficient, grudging, and none too appetizing.

However, with Father by her side helping her prepare dishes for dinner and for special feast days, she turned out masterpieces of *chung* (or *zongzi*), triangular, bamboo-wrapped, glutinous rice traditionally served during the annual Dragon Boat festival to celebrate the sacrificial drowning of Qu Yuan, a mythic patriot protesting an emperor's ill-fated policies. Above all, she was the supreme mistress of popiah, the delicate original of the egg roll, a delicious wrap of paper-thin skins of steamed rice flour, rolled with diced yellow bean curd, shrimp, sprouts, and jicama, boiled to a rich filling with pork lard.

All this chopping, frying, wrapping took place in the back enclosure of a small house, without my involvement, for I shunned my Second Mother's example. Like my luckless mother, she appeared to be a creature of fate. My mother had escaped domestic drudgery, only to find unhappiness as a single woman working in Singapore City. Second Mother was wholly immersed in housework and child care, a more dreary end I could not imagine, a misfortune enacted before me daily. Cooking, the one talent that was boasted about women in Malaysian society, did nothing for women's satisfaction, as far as I could see.

Yet my contempt for cooking went hand in hand with my horrible sense of inferiority at my physical incompetence. That I had no idea even how to cook rice, or to launder a dress, or sew a zipper into a skirt went together with my role as a student. After the Third Form Exams for the nationally administered Lower Certificate, Father went to town clutching the printed parchment that bore the number of A's I had received. Such academic success excused me from mere women's work. Brains marked me as privileged, and privilege made me the equal of my brothers. I always had a book in hand. Father came home from work and helped Second Mother. He dusted, mopped, swept the floors, ironed our clothes, and washed the dishes. The only daughter, I read and read and read. Father partitioned poverty so that he and Second Mother bore the brunt of labor, while we children with our Mandarin promise were to be the engines pulling the family back into the class status of our wealthy ancestors. Labor was for the failures; Father saw his children as already successful.

The first time I ever cooked a dish is vivid in my mind for the poverty of the dish and for the powerful jolt of independence that came with making it. It was the first time I used my hands to materialize a thing that I could eat, and of course it could not take place in Second Mother's kitchen. In fact, I have never cooked in Second Mother's kitchen. The territorial taboo has been too deeply embedded to dispel.

Chiew, a classmate, lived the next street over, in a row of bungalows that appeared the acme of comfort and security contrasted to our wood frame shack. We were twelve years old, only a few years ahead of the age when we had played at pretend meals, *masak-masak,* with clay and grass clippings. On most Saturdays, Chiew and I shared books and school talk, but that afternoon, we decided to have a real adventure. We decided to cook something. At the corner all-purpose store, I bought *ikan bilis,* dried salted anchovies, for ten cents, all the money I possessed. Chiew's mother's kitchen was clean, an actual separate room at the back of the bungalow. It had a kerosene stove with two burners. Looking through the larder, we found a bottle of peanut oil, sugar, and chilies.

Here is the recipe as I recall it. We turned the burner high and set the seasoned kwali or wok on it. When the teaspoon of peanut oil was hot in the wok, I threw in one long chili pepper, seeds and all, chopped up roughly, which browned almost immediately. Quickly I put in all the *ikan bilis* my ten cents had bought, about half a cup remaining after I had picked off and discarded the heads. I tossed the anchovies and the chili pieces together in the hot oil, then added a tablespoon of sugar. The dish was ready in under ten minutes, the anchovies fried brown and crisp from the sugar and burning hot in the mouth from the chilies.[1]

It was a simple dish, as inexpensive and speedy as Second Mother's dishes; but I fancied I had invented it, made it spontaneously out of what was there in Chiew's kitchen, with the taste of salt, sweet, and hot, still my favorite taste combination today. The strong sense of power I felt running through my body that afternoon from the act of cooking, of making food rather than waiting for it to arrive or not arrive from another human, a food stall, or a peddler, was a new sensation. In place of the usual imagined excitement mined from the blank pauses that had me turning page after page after page of novels, till my eyes burned and the Saturday had nudged reluctantly to a close, this elation felt real. That I could make even as simple a dish as fried chilies and anchovies was remarkable to me. The physical work, small as it was, confirmed a material self, a self that Mother's abandonment, Father's pressures on academic achievement, Second Mother's silence and neglect, and my own obsessive reading had almost wholly turned immaterial, a waif of too much misery and too much mind.

That moment clicked a number of fragmented puzzles into place for me: the marvelous feeling of unalienated labor together with the imperative to work with my hands on things, to flesh out and vivify the gray cloudy shadows of mentality. Outside the examples of mothers, playing at cooking, I learned the power in this woman-identified act: an act in which the material and the symbolic correspond exactly; the motive and the body one and the same.

Note

[1] Here is the recipe for the dish, so simple that even a child can make it.

Chilies and Dried Anchovies (*Ikan Bilis Pedas*)
Cooking time: about 10 minutes

Ingredients:
4 ounces of dried anchovies (*ikan bilis*)
4 tablespoons peanut oil
2–4 dried chilies (depending on spiciness preferred)
1 clove garlic
1 tablespoon sugar
1/4 cup hot water
6 ounces peanuts (optional)

Place dried chilies in hot water till soft. Then drain and pound chilies with garlic to paste. Avoid contact with hands and especially with eyes!

Pick through the anchovies and remove heads and other extraneous material.

Heat the peanut oil and fry the anchovies whole until crispy brown. Make sure they do not burn. Using a slotted spoon, remove and place on paper towels to drain.

Fry the chili paste in hot oil for about three minutes and add sugar, stirring constantly to prevent burning. Add peanuts and anchovies and fry for about two minutes.

Serve as an appetizer or snack. It's especially good with beer.

Mother Is Converting the Church with Eggrolls

Oliver de la Paz

This crowd has cravings. Churchgoers, the faithful,
flock to the fragrance, fried eggrolls.
They eat eagerly. With the ease of breaking
bread, she blesses, builds more
magnificent manna. The men worship
the wisdom of the wok; the whorls of oil
open, obedient. The organic grease
gurgles and gasps and the gas stove
sears the snacks. Sputter and hiss,
the howl of hunger, heats the normally
neighborly. Their need for nourishment increases.

Insatiable, the incense of the immaculate air
is absorbed by admirers. The allegro of the ravenous
reaches her ritual. They roar with loss,
the last log. But like loaves and fishes,
fifteen, fifty, five hundred
hidden halves are heated. The befuddled
bite into beneficence, a blessing on the tongues
of twenty or thirty. The theologians push,
priests of the parish, they pass the salmon
with shallot sauce, the spicy meatloaf,
and march to my mother, their mania, their devotion.

- food made into a kind of religion
- connecting other people
- affecting appreciation of one person

My Father's Pho

Kim Ly Bui-Burton

The broth is always steaming when I arrive;
oxtail-scented mist,
the way mornings began in his childhood,
fog rising off the Mekong,
the soup vendor's cart close behind.

Pale half moons of onion, *oignon*,
that word the French forced on his tongue.
Ordered piles of beef:
"meat is a seasoning, not a meal."
Coriander's leafy green.

He remembers that color steeping the hills.
Adds rice sticks, bleached as the stalks
harvested after American rain.
White *ao dai*, white bones.
The noodles curl thick in the pot.

All this my father gives me:
memory's meat, the salt of *nuoc mam*
and grief, heat of soup, his lost life.
He finishes with the sweetness of lime.
The first bowl is mine. I will eat.

Presence

Anh Quynh Bui

I bring fruit and milk to the morning corner—
golden cherry clusters and sour plums,
slate-filmed grapes with pits
mangoes instead of apples, blood tangerines
and dried kumquats instead of raisins

I feel the sweet gloss over my tongue, hiding in my cheek crevices, biting into the tooth enamel, where only four years ago a blunt cavity waged a war. Stretching so that my shirt rises from the bulge, I feel the sun and shelter my eyes from the heat. Boiled strawberries taste like spoiled jam. Warm kiwis smell of slug-covered roads crossed by cars on a rainy night. Wet-fleshed bananas, long brown, creep through my organs too slowly to escape the hot afternoon flush. Salt avocados and green lemons make up for these things until the evening sun carries the day back. The space for consumption is too large. It needs to be folded up, not intricately, just compactly. I am not asking for balletic demonstrations or orderly grotesqueries, just a minor crumpling so that the white-veined surfaces where all those days are written don't show; no one will read my excesses.

At night, I dream of compressed cream and children who follow me from bed. I want to believe and split lemons with my thumbs and maybe eat an oyster or two without flinching. And then I want to resist, settle my stomach. A bicarbonate bubbles through my nose, while the soothing strains of rushing water pacify my head. Early-hour dreams turn water into gold. Of course, the morning leaves me wondering what confidences remain. Old friends don't wrap their presents as such. They know there are no surprises left.

Rice

Aurora Harris

In our Armenian, Jewish, Negro
mixed-race neighborhood
at five years old
before writing with pencil
when Dr. Seuss was El Rey[1]
I was taught how to cook
the two-times-a-day dish
affectionately known as
"Is There More Rice?"

— words in language of heritage pertain to food + family

I stood on a chair
in front of the sink
with mama's Tagalog
mi abuelo's[2] Castilian—
bigas y arroth and
papa's "No butter,
no sugar is good."
I washed the rice three times—

hinogasang ko ang bigas.[3]
I washed the rice twice
in a scarred metal pot
that put stories of slavery and wars
in their mouths.
I washed the rice once—
milky starch disappeared
and the water was clear
enough for their eyes.

I measured the water
according to digits
of my middle finger
this was better than cups
and easier to use.

Mi abuelo would transfer
the pot to the fire—
I napped to Naciemento for cuarenta minutos[4]
while sambas boiled
and lowered the flame,
and when I woke up
arroth-bigas-rice-lutong-kanin[5]
with fish heads and squid
was ready to eat.

They'd tell me that I
was a wonderful cook
while I ate with my fingers
instead of a fork
and thought about cooking
the next evening's meal . . .
I decided on seaweed,
Uncle Chico's red snapper,
arroth-bigas-rice, beans
"More rice."
"Sí, there's rice."

Notes

[1] El Rey (Spanish)—the king.
[2] mi abuelo (Spanish)—grandfather.
[3] hinogasang ko ang bigas (Tagalog)—I washed the rice.
[4] cuarenta minutos (Spanish)—forty minutes.
[5] lutong kanin (Tagalog)—cooked rice.

Making Marmalade

BeeBee Tan-Beck

The season comes round again
when wax ducks and mandarins abound,
when you and Beautiful Sweetheart
wield ever so lightly the razor-
keen cleavers, to shape exquisite
strips of white and orange
roots into delicate blooms.
Two sisters competing
for what effect other than to please
Grandma's demanding palate?

Mother, how can I begin
to challenge the paper-thin
slices of turnips and carrots
or the store-bought perfection
of amber sweetness captured
in a jar of thick cut Sevilles
and whiskey that father favors?

And though I want to be the perfect
daughter who makes the perfect marmalade,
the perfect mother and the perfect wife
churning out the fulfillment of your chamber
dreams, what I saw
in the carefully cut citrus
was all too easily melted down,
the sticky syrup of self
delusion boiled over
and uneasily set in the life
I recarve with sharpened
Blades of poetry.

Love and Gender

You Bring Out the Vietnamese Woman in Me

Ahn Phuong-Nguyen

*After Sandra Cisneros's "You Bring Out
the Mexican in Me"*

You bring out the Vietnamese woman in me.
The hand-to-hand mines.
The jungle fear of jungle fever.
The wasted war.
The cold coconut on the way from Bien Hoa
to Vung Tau.
You are the one I'd sip time with,
dine and unwind without
fear and evening wear,
even in monsoon weather
One day. Someday.

With you.

You bring out the *con gai* in me.
The New Year dragon in me.
The soft *tinh*, tint of pink in me.
The lotus blossom floating aways in me.
The Pacific Rim in me.
The undulating waves in me.
The vultures and doves in me.
The *Saigon Oi* of the blood in me.
The *Sino-French* taste of love in me.
The certainty of tongue in me.
The *de thuong,* de yeu in me.
The *Kieu* morality in me.
The boat passage and impasses in me.
The migrant diaspora, refugee camps in me.
The years of neglect in me.
Yes, you too. Yes, you too.

You bring out the American in me.
The consumerism of desire in me.
The stock market crash of '29 in me.
The *Roe v. Wade* in me.
The Sexual Revolution in me.
The Barbie romance in me.
The long Sunday drive in me.
The makeup the camera with film in me.

Boyfriend. My distant other,
I am the dream that crumples your bed sheets
that folds you tight as shadow folds night.
I claim you as mine,
as long as freedom rings.
I want to ravish and relish you in twin.
I want to defile you and open graves.
I want to wake the dead with screaming,
shrill and soft, and slice the dark with knives.
Em la Nguoi Viet Hai Ngoai,
like it or not, sweetheart.

You bring out the Vietcong in me.
The do what we do even if it's wrong in me.
The grenade in palm in me.
The untrained assassin in me.
The *Ngay Tet* disaster in me.
The orange fever in me
The pacifist monk in me.
I could immolate myself in the name of you and feel
it worth it. Torch the tires and terrorize rivals,
female and male, who linger and lust for you,
late in your life. Oh,

I am envy. I am the peacock with a thousand eyes.
I am the seer of men.
The explicit solicitor without consent.
The dreamer's scheming. You bring out
the sadistic potential in me.
The exotic differential in me.
The absolute and circumstantial truth in me.
The original question in me.

Sea *xanh*. Blue *xanh*. Indigo. *Ao dai.*
Hoa giay. Opal. Peach spray. Pearl.
All you saints, blessed and laid,
Duc Me. Theresa.
I invoke you.

Anh voi em. Always two. Always together.
Anh yeu em. Hon roi. Hon doi.
Love the way a Vietnamese man loves a woman. Let
me know you. Love the other way around I'll show you.

Smoke

Chachoua Victoria Xiong

The late-afternoon sunlight beamed through the dirty windows of an old Philadelphia apartment in January. The young woman squinted as she looked at the young man sleeping beside her on the dusty mattress on the floor. They slept naked as usual, and confined in such a small apartment, tucked far away from their past, the young woman smiled with contentment. She watched as he began to move. With one eye half-open, he saw she was already awake.

"What are you doing?" he croaked.

"Riding a bike," she said with a smile. She kissed him on the lips and lay on top of him under three thin comforters. He began to move from under her to get up, but as his skin met the chilly air, he squirmed back under her.

"What happened to the heater?" he protested.

She touched his stubbled cheeks and drawled, "I'm as content as a cow chewing its cud on a grassy hill." His long blond hair was a little oily; she played with it between her fingers, braided a portion of it.

"We better get up if we want to drive to Bronxville before night," he said.

"Yeah, yeah, yeah. *Bpth!*" she sputtered. She trapped his arms and legs with her hands and knees. "You get up first."

He struggled free from under her. Soon, he was sitting on top of her with her arms pinned down. He kissed her lightly, and they were immediately consumed with each other, immersed in sharing and giving. He held her face in his hands, gazed at her lips, dark hair, dark eyes. His lips barely grazed hers as he whispered, "I love you."

◆ ◆ ◆

She showered first, as usual, since it took her longer to get ready, and he began breakfast. The kitchen was just a counter with a sink and a stove in the corner of the apartment, and the refrigerator stood solidly right inside their living area. He broke two eggs in a small bowl and mixed in milk and brown sugar. Then he heated up the

100

skillet and soaked the bread in the egg mixture. The stove warmed up the small apartment quickly.

Breakfast was the only meal he liked to cook. She made dinner because she knew how to improvise with their meager canned and dry goods. Their cupboards were filled with ramen noodles, tuna, ravioli, chicken noodle soup, beans, egg noodles, and popcorn. Such was the menu for students.

When she finished showering, she left the water running so the bathroom would be warm for him. She cleaned up in the kitchen while he took a ten-minute shower. They'd been together two years, and their morning routine was like clockwork. Like any young relationship, they were in the sweet and altruistic stage.

She sliced up a banana that would've been thrown out by the end of the day. They ate from the same plate. Shared the same glass of milk. They did this for two reasons: because it made them feel romantic and because it saved them cleanup time.

"Know what always happens to me whenever I drink milk?" he said.

"You finish it?"

"I always get to the bottom of the glass, and then I'll still have one more bite left of whatever I'm eating, but I run out of milk! It always happens, no matter how much I pour."

"Then why don't you pour more than you think you'll need?"

"Because I hate tossing milk. I have to drink it all up, but then I can't eat without milk. Then when I get more milk, I always pour too much!"

"It's milk! Who cares. I'll drink whatever's left, *sheesh*. And if I can't finish it, just pretend that I'm not throwing it away, Okay?"

When he reached his last bite of French toast, true enough, all the milk was gone. So she went to the monster refrigerator and poured enough for one swallow.

"There. See? It's perfect," she said.

"But the glass was empty. It's still irritating! The milk was gone," he complained. She smiled, walked to the sink, and watched his face contort into horror as she slowly poured the milk down the sink.

"Nooo!" he hollered in melodramatic agony.

After they cleaned the dishes and dressed, they put their coats on to bulk up for the cold outside. His car was parked two blocks from the apartment in a lot next to an Amoco station on Broad Street. It was blue-cold out. Cars sludged through dirty snow; the sun had almost disappeared from the horizon.

"You want to drive, or should I?" she said as they spotted his tan Taurus.

"I'll drive," he said. They settled themselves inside the car for their three-hour trip to Bronxville. They drove back and forth between Philadelphia and Bronxville because he went to college and worked in Philadelphia, and they shared an apartment in both cities.

Far away from home, they felt like two adventurers exploring new places, collecting memories, making their mark on the world. Etched on the sidewalk somewhere in downtown Philadelphia, their initials were inscribed inside a rough outline of a heart: "LS + JF." They were always together. They didn't make friends. They shared a secret that tied them closer than any ring, ceremony, or vow. They were safe in their world and seldom left their apartments except to shuttle from one to the other.

In the car, they listened to one of her favorite CDs by the Pat Metheny Group.

"The reason why you hate Pedro is because he can sing higher than you," she said.

"I don't sing, and if I did I wouldn't want to sing that high. No real man could sing that high."

"He's not! He can't be."

"He is. Just listen to him." He began to mock Pedro in falsetto, lisping and fluttering his eyelashes.

"Christ, when you do it that way . . ." She laughed.

They were on the New Jersey Turnpike and one hour away from her apartment. To their right, the Empire State Building marked the splendid Manhattan skyline, the Hudson glistening like onyx in the forefront. The turnpike was dark and nearly empty.

Suddenly, a violent thump of something heavy landed on top of the car and the windshield caved in. She watched him squeeze his eyes shut, bracing himself for impact. He inhaled deeply as though it were his last breath and stood on the brakes. Bits of glass flew everywhere. The car stopped.

"It was a person!" he shouted. He looked to the rear of the car and reversed it a few feet. She was stunned to see the shattered glass all over her lap, the dashboard, his shoulders and hair. The thump sounded like they'd hit a large pothole. They must have crashed into a road barrel. Cars continued to whiz past.

He jumped out and ran toward the mound in the middle of the turnpike. She stepped hesitantly in his direction. "Come back. Don't go there. What is it?" Her voice sounded hollow.

Something like clothing fluttered from the mound. Smoke rose from it. Suddenly the cold seemed colder, the night darker, the cars seemed to drive slower.

He ran back and put his arm around her, "She's dead."

"How do you know?"

"I can tell, okay?"

"What was it?" she whispered, dazed.

"She ran in front of the car. I didn't see her until she was right there. It was a girl."

They hurried back inside the car.

"Let's go," he said. In panic, he started the engine and shifted into first gear. They wanted to drive away. They wanted to pretend that it hadn't happened. By driving away, they would erase the accident, undo it.

"Okay," she said, "but look." The windshield on his side was scattered in piles on the dashboard, the floor. They both stared at the ugly hole and up into the clear Jersey night and slowly realized that they were still alive.

"Are you hurt?" she asked, beginning to cry. "Are you all right?"

He examined himself quickly, "I'm okay." She looked at his hands, his face. They had both worn their winter coats and had had their seatbelts on. Their bodies were unscathed. She glared as cars drove by innocent, trouble free. Why they were chosen out of all the cars passively driving by?

They went outside again. The man waved his arms at the cars and trucks driving by. A trucker stopped. By now the young woman was sobbing.

"It's okay. We didn't get hurt. We're going to be all right," the young man said.

The trucker approached the young couple. "You folks all right? What happened?"

After the young man told him, the trucker put his arm around the young woman and said, "You're going to be all right. This happens all the time. Everything's going to be okay. I'll radio the police."

A few spectators parked their cars on the shoulder and peered at the dead girl on the highway. Cars sped by, some inches away from the body. The young woman watched as what looked like smoke steamed off the mound of flesh.

In a few minutes, New Jersey state patrol cars lined the road, blocking all but one lane. In the backseat of one of the patrol cars they gave their account of what happened. From where they sat, the headlights of the car beamed garishly on the dead girl. She was wearing a red parka that had mercifully blown over her crushed head. Underneath, she was naked except for a white G-string. Her skin was waxy and white, almost blue, and her body was so flat it seemed to be part of the road and not a body. Her legs were abnormally short because they had broken off upon impact. That was the source of the steam escaping from her body into the cold night.

"I didn't even see her. She just came running out of nowhere," said the young man. He was pale and shivering. Bits of glass were still stuck in his hair.

"When did you first see her?" asked the officer.

"I first saw her when she was right in front of my headlights." His teeth began to chatter.

The officer looked at the young woman. "Did you see what happened?"

"No, I didn't see any of it. I was doing something to the radio. I looked down for one second to do something to the radio, and then it happened." She clung to the young man's arm. She examined her hands and his, and began crying again when she saw that a piece of glass had cut into his left palm. "You're hurt," she whispered.

"Okay, do either of you need an ambulance? Are you guys hurt?" asked the officer.

"No," the man said quickly. "We didn't get hurt."

The officer wrote something on a clipboard. "Do you want the heater turned up?"

"Yes," they said. Soon the officer finished what he was writing and left the car to talk to other officers. The young man and woman shivered and held each other inside the car. They were growing exhausted.

"Do you think it's a sign?" he said when the car warmed them up.

"What do you mean?" she asked.

"Because of what we did to Leslie."

"What? How could she have anything to do with it?"

"She e-mailed me something about paying child support and something about cursing us both."

"You think Leslie cursed us? Does she know how?"

"She had a friend at work who was into witchcraft. She was interested in it, but I thought she was just trying to scare me. Think she would do it?"

"Yeah, I think she would. I think she's that angry. I know my sister. Leslie doesn't let grudges go, ever," said the woman. "What are you thinking?"

"Nothing. Maybe she's right. Maybe what we're doing is wrong," he said.

"You can't let her do that to you. I love you. There's nothing wrong with that!" she cried. "And you love me, don't you? *Don't you?* This accident doesn't have anything to do with us."

"Yes. Yes, I do. You're right."

The officer drove them to the young woman's apartment. He assured them everything would be fine, that people foolishly tried to cross the turnpike all the time. When they reached her building, the couple thanked him and walked slowly inside. They didn't speak to each other. They took off their coats and clothes and went to bed. With the lights off, the woman said, "Do you think she's with us?"

"Who?"

"That gir—"

"No."

"I've heard that spirits linger around their killers before they lea—"

"We didn't kill her," he said. Then he rolled over, turning his back to her.

The woman thought for a moment. She knew the way he handled things. The way he shut down his feelings and shut out thoughts and pushed away anything that bothered him. He would do this until he could forget.

"You're going to leave me, aren't you?" she said.

Colloquial Love

Anh Quynh Bui

I learned from a woman who would know, claiming, as she did, to have worked as a phone sex operator for six months, that there are certain words that will trigger desire no matter how they are strung together. Men do not need a narrative to become aroused, only the ringing of certain bells. Like so many dogs they pant and bulge. It's not a science, but then it's not really an art, she says.

I don't let her show me.

By 4 A.M., we slouch in taped-up beanbags, passing a single beer. She hands it to me while its mouth is still warm from her lips, wordlessly offering to wipe it clean. When I shake my head no, she shows me a trick she learned in third grade when a lice scare produced a corollary concern about shared soda cans. Pour out a little first; the stream of soda washes away the spit germs. I ask her if she cleaned the operator headsets where she used to work. She laughs, but tells me that one Corrine G. carried a big bottle of 409 and a roll of paper towels in her handbag. Every day, before and after work, she cleaned every inch of her station, easing twisted up bits of paper in and out of corners that she couldn't see. All the half-words that floated around that gray-walled room, all the moaning and sighing and aroused exhalations, all those lying noises, gave the place a visible grit, though Corrine would never say such a thing.

We talk about colloquial love.
We divide the body into regions, list the vernacular demanded by certain touches and semantic problems caused by roving hands. We map sighs onto skin, we put on accents.

She claimed that sex was not meant to be quiet.
And this complaint was all too familiar. He asks for words at first and then, when I cannot not oblige, my mind too busy building fantasies about better places, better lovers, better beds, and unwilling to describe them, all the wrong words come to me—something

about faces and love, black-corner rendezvous and distance. Expressions of lust strung together in the moment of desire lose their straight-face charm. Coherence is too thoughtful. Spoken sentences too time-consuming.

And yet the eager fall of sounds he pitches aims for my breasts, my full belly and my thighs. These notes confuse me, which are meant to be my own, which are his, all summoned by some demand for exclamation.

Quiet love
Discomfits my memory
Most nights, my body still weighted with being beneath him though he is long gone, I give my ear to other sounds. Conversations about cars and wanderlust float to the second-story windows, hover there. I brush his low voice aside and arch my back, strain to hear the traffic. Public transportation is the most insistent; occasionally a bike will skid. Airplane rumbles twist the night air into unrequited condolences. Later, drowsy yet, I imagine I can hear the clockwork stars moving like traffic lights, blinking with the sounds of the regular world. Engulfed in such arousals, it is not hard to feel the moving world echo your own breathing. At last wordless and easy.

Finding Touch: A Personal Essay

Noel Alumit

"Will the parents of a boy wearing brown corduroy pants and a blue vest come to the entrance?"

I'm three. I'm lost.

"Will the parents of a boy wearing jeans and a striped shirt come to the main register?"

I get lost a lot. At the zoo, the department stores, parks, museums, the city of New York. I don't do it on purpose. I'm curious and adventurous. Why is the elephant's nose so long? I wonder what would happen if Snoopy played with the other dolls. There are probably worms in the bushes. Go and find out.

"Will the parents of a boy wearing a green sweater come to the information desk? He's crying . . . and we can't make him stop . . . *please* come—immediately!"

I cry, howl. The world can be intimidating when all you see is legs. I cry because I know my parents will be pissed. They have other children to care for. Having to stop their trip to find me is not pleasant.

"Again, Noel?" Mama says, shaking her head, her hands on her hips. A Lost Cause, she seems to be saying.

"If you get lost again, we're not going to come and find you," Dad says, a snarl plastered onto his face. "You can live with the wallets in Lost and Found."

My parents tie a leash to me, a piece of rope that goes around my chest. It doesn't hurt, but it stays on me wherever we go. It comes off when I enter school.

I come home to find my mother. Dad is working. When day ends, Dad comes home, then Mom disappears. She is working. Mom is a nurse. Dad is a cashier.

♦ ♦ ♦

I turn nine. I'm one of a handful of Filipinos, in a busload of black children, to be bused into Bel-Air. Something about integration. We're late to school because the driver gets lost in the Bel-Air mountains.

We're caught in mist, above and below, a billowing whiteness. And I think of how we're resting in God's beard. The only thing missing is angels.

From the back of the bus, a kid points to a shellacked home with a huge picture window. I see inside. Plants and paintings are against a white wall. Someone yells from behind me, "That's the house that Farrah Fawcett lives in."

Mom is a nurse. Dad is a janitor.

♦ ♦ ♦

At school, the black girls, like Sharon and Renee, find a corner of the yard and make up dance steps. The white girls, like Becky and Lisa, watch. Mr. Morton takes us into the school auditorium and teaches us square dancing. Mr. Morton knows the dances real well. I don't think he's married.

I'm hanging with the black boys. They talk about *What's Happenin'* and *Good Times.* I'm hanging with the white boys. One boy tells me how his father is the producer of a TV show I watch all the time. Glenn is the only other Filipino boy I know. We don't talk about anything.

Mom is a nurse. Dad puts candy into vending machines.

♦ ♦ ♦

In ninth grade, a computer glitch lands me on the cross-country running class. I don't particularly care for the sport, but I'm chubby. Actually, I'm fat. I take being put on the running team as a sign from God that I need to lose weight. So I don't change the error.

I train with the team for a whole semester. Training requires running from school to Elysian Park. Then back to school. I am always the last one in—not because I'm the slowest, although being slow is a factor, but because I can't remember how to get back.

At home, Dad prepares to go to work. He wears his brown security guard uniform. A lock of his hair escapes his well-pomaded head, falling across his left brow. It touches his gold-rimmed glasses. The gold matches the badge of his uniform. I want to say something to him, but don't know what. Something important. Something meaningful. Something beyond, "How was school?" I'm his son, and he's my father, so something must be said at some point, right? I'm fourteen, and words don't come easy.

I continue to run. I lose fifteen pounds.

◆ ◆ ◆

When I'm in college, my father moves back to the Philippines. I forget to write. So does he. Words never come. A cousin of mine uses Dad's phone to make long-distance phone calls to the States. He runs up an astronomical phone bill. My father refuses to pay it. It remains disconnected. We lose touch. Are you living with the wallets?

◆ ◆ ◆

I audition for school plays. There is one play I want to do very badly. It is called *As Is* by William M. Hoffman. It's a play about gay men. I'm eventually cast. I identify with the characters.

I meet a boy named Steve. We kiss in the darkness of my bedroom. I solidify a part of myself that I'd suspected for a long time. The next day Steve tells me he's straight and was only experimenting. I look for him around campus.

I find him. He's with his new girlfriend.

Mom is a nurse.

◆ ◆ ◆

I get my degree in acting. After college, Mom suggests I be more active. With no school structure to dictate my life, I have lots of time. I join the church choir to prove to God I'm a good Catholic.

I sing, losing myself in hymns hundreds of years old, staring at the emaciated corpse of a God. We hover behind the parishioners like angels. We watch them solemnly bow their heads.

I have a memory. It is of my father. His head is bowed. It is always bowed, his eyes cast to the ground. "It's a good way of finding lost change," he said.

I do volunteer work for a nearby hospice. I'm told being gay is a sin. If I commit acts of kindness, like caring for the dying, maybe God will cancel out the sin.

◆ ◆ ◆

I'm auditioning. I sit in a waiting room filled with other young Asian men. I'm one of the many heads the casting director looks over. She calls someone's name to read for her.

I know I'm not going to get the part, because it requires heavy duty martial arts skills. My résumé says I can tap-dance. I go off into a corner and practice my generic Asian accent for the role. Asian accents were never my specialty in voice class. I try to remember how my father sounded, but I can't.

♦ ♦ ♦

"Please don't do this to me," he says.

I'm surprised. Sam rarely speaks. Just sings. Broadway tunes mostly. He is small. With hair the color of fire.

He's nicknamed the Wanderer. He shuffles down the halls of the hospice, turning left, right, up stairs, down stairs, into the parking lot out front, the trees near by. I follow him because it is my responsibility to see that he doesn't hurt himself. On our treks, we sing Sondheim.

I do most of the talking. I speak to him. About anything. I make up things. And when I can't think of anything else, silence. It isn't a deep silence, uniting us. It is empty and uneasy, the result of having nothing left to say.

He stares blankly at me. I stare at the clock on the wall, wondering if I could skip out of my volunteer work early.

"Please don't do this to me."

Dementia has eaten the insides of his brain, leaving him here, leaving him far away. But for a moment, he is back; a slight chemical connection in his brain forces him to return and see what is going on.

He sees what he is going through, what people are doing to him, how he is living. He hears the nurses and the doctors and the volunteers talk to him as if he were a five-year-old, instead of the thirty-something man that he is. He remembers having to be spoon-fed, with drool racing to stain his shirt. He feels the diaper around his waist.

To all of us, to all of it, he says, in a delicate whimper, "Please don't do this to me."

The chemical connection falters. He is gone again. Wandering . . .

I discover bars. Dim and smoky. Colored lights move here and there. Every once in a while, a red strobe light finds me, hitting me in the chest. I wander around with a where-could-my-friends-have-gone look on my face to disguise the fact that I came alone because I have no other gay friends. I wonder what my father would think.

I eventually meet Frank. A friend. Just a friend. We pal around together. Have a few dinners and have a few beers. He's from Australia.

◆ ◆ ◆

Sam dies.

"He transitioned," somebody said.

I go to the bars again. To find someone. Anyone.

◆ ◆ ◆

I tell Frank about Sam. He sympathizes.

"You wanna go out?" he asks. Frank's voice is eternally wispy. With his long blond hair falling over his face, he reminds me of a nymph or a fairy—a real storybook fairy.

"Yeah, let's go out," I say.

We drive around Silverlake in my jeep, the top down. Like it was meant to be. Getting whistles from guys. More for Frank than for me. His blond hair blows in the wind, like Farrah Fawcett's.

Sam fades from my mind.

I'm twenty-four. I'm realizing what it means to be a gay man. A bachelor forever. The memory of dead friends can disappear with a mad dash on the town.

We stop at a Chinese restaurant and have red wine. When we're done, we start walking to my car, parked a block away. It's not even midnight yet. What else can we do?

Frank and I stop at a curb. A white pickup comes our way. We wait for it to pass. It stops. It doesn't move. A bunch of guys, maybe six, sit in the truck looking at us funny.

I grew up in the inner city. I know what a bunch of guys looking at you funny means. I don't know if gang bangers look the same Down Under.

From the front seat, I hear someone say, "Get 'em."

Before any of those guys jump out of the truck, I yell, "RUUU-UUUUN!!!"

I've seen the signs around the neighborhood that says gay bashers have been spotted in the neighborhood. Gay men are encouraged to walk in pairs and report any suspicious-looking men. I pass one of the flyers stapled to the telephone pole when I take off.

"Fucking faggot!" a voice screams behind me. I'm thinking of cross-country class. We were instructed to sprint the closer we got to the finish line. I always looked behind me to see if I was the last one. I turn around. A guy's after me. Maybe it is the moonlight or the lamplight that helps me see the knife get closer to my back. The metal is bright, like a torch. I think of the Olympics and how they were held in Los Angeles in 1984.

I have never run in boots before. I'm running. I'm running as fast as I can, competing with wind. Run, run, run. Faster, faster, faster. If I focus on my breathing, and stare straight ahead, I can run forever. There's a high that occurs when your heart pumps. Sweat falls from your body like tears needing to be shed. Let me get there. Let me. Please, Sir, let me. I'll be free if I can just go fast enough. Faster. He's still behind me. A few inches is all he needs. Oh, God please, let me get away. I'm turning left, then turning right, up and down streets, remembering the halls that Sam wandered.

Please don't do this to me, I think to myself.

Somehow I'm alone. I get away. I thought Frank would be with me. But he's not. I run back. They have Frank against the wall. They're beating him. Frank's a dancer. I've seen him leap and suspend himself in the air like a cloud. But he's against a fence. There's no way he could fly now.

"Get the fuck away from him!!!" I yell and charge toward them. Some wore scapulars, religious vestments no bigger than an inch that hang around your neck. I owned a scapular once. When I received my first Holy Communion, I was given one with a rosary. Catholic boys. The guys in the truck are Catholic. We may have shared a mass together.

"Get the fuck away from him!!!"

One of the gang guys hears me, he's after me. I'm dodging him as he tries to attack me. I should have studied Tae Kwon Do like my brother. Like my sister.

More people come to the street. The gang guys disperse. I'm wondering what to do. I go to Frank. He's shaking but all right. There seem to be no visible marks on him.

We go to the police and tell them we were just attacked. The receptionist tells us the attack happened in another district and to fill out a report at the precinct there. We drive. We make out the report. We neglect to call it a hate crime. We don't go to the hospital. Why make the evening longer?

I drive Frank home to Hollywood. We pass a building where my father used to be a security guard. Frank tells me one of the guys tried to stab him. It was a switchblade. The knife folded when it hit his leg. He thanks God. God was watching out for me, he says. He wouldn't know what to do if one of his legs were injured. I think of the computer glitch that put me in cross-country class, teaching me how to run. But I don't thank God.

Later, Frank and I try to forget what happened. We talk less and less. We lose touch. Forgotten.

Also later, I quit the choir. I don't feel like singing anymore.

I feel an invisible rope pulling me home. And I'm lost. My mother sleeps alone. And I'm lost. I sit in the bedroom that I grew up in. I look around. I bury my head into my hands. Tears fall. And I'm lost. Will the parents of a boy . . . In the darkness, I scream with a voice that only I can hear. *Find me find me someone please find me.*

♦ ♦ ♦

I might drive to the beach and stand at that great In-Between known as the Pacific Ocean. I might look out and realize that a part of me lives on an island somewhere out there. I might hear that my father had a heart attack. I might see pictures of him not looking the way I remembered. My mother might bring him home.

Mom is a nurse. Dad is a patient.

Dad and I might sit silently. I might try to make the silence unempty. I might look at him while he falls asleep, finding touch. I might wonder what to say when he wakes.

A Day at the A&P

Kay Vu-Lee

It was a hot, humid summer in 1977. My parents didn't know how to drive yet, so we biked over to Arbor Land Mall, on Washtenaw Avenue, the main strip in Ann Arbor, just off of Highway 23. We lived on Lillian Street, a couple of miles from the University of Michigan. In our quiet neighborhood lived doctors, lawyers, and dogs. I feared dogs and avoided going outside. I lived in our backyard, on the swings and around my mom's pumpkin patch. Our church gave me an old sturdy blue tricycle that I rode up and down our garage entrance; my parents had bicycles that took them farther.

During our first summer in America, my father came home from Weber's Inn and learned how to ride the old green rusty bike that St. Luke's Lutheran Church had given us. As refugees, we were sponsored by one of St. Luke's members. The church played a large part in our transition from the refugee camp to America. They found a house for our family of seven: Grandpa, Grandma, Aunt Lo, Dad, Mom, myself, and Pheng. The church members even furnished it for us, filled the refrigerator with food, and hung clothes in our closets. They even put a recliner in the den for Grandpa. There wasn't a car in the garage because Dad couldn't drive yet, so he learned how to ride the bike.

I loved that old hand-me-down bike. It had a little wire basket hooked on the front, and I wished that I were big enough to ride the big metal horse. The places I could go and all the new things I could explore! I wished my parents weren't so uptight and would let me go out more often.

When Dad tried to ride the bicycle for the first time, he looked ridiculous, like he was having a convulsion while trying to pedal. His toes bled because he got them stuck in the chain, and he fell on the cement sidewalk. Mom tried to soothe his pain by yelling at him.

"Why is it that an old person like you can't ever do anything right?" she yelled, her face all scrunched up.

"I was just trying to learn how to ride this bike, and before I knew it, my toes were bleeding," Dad said, bending over his foot.

"Only you!" barked Mom from the kitchen.

Mom wanted to show Dad that she was more coordinated. A few days later, she decided to hop on the bike. She, too, came home with a bloody toe. Mom's forgotten how to ride now, but Dad still remembers, though it takes him a few minutes to balance himself each time he gets on.

It was really hot that day in Ann Arbor, and we needed to buy groceries. Our sponsors were busy, so we decided to go shopping at Arbor Land where there was an A&P. I wanted to protest against Pheng coming with us. He was only three years old, but if I said anything, I would be left behind with my grandparents. Because I was a girl and he a boy, I knew he came first. I didn't want to jeopardize my only chance of getting out that day.

We biked and walked in the hot August sun on white bright glittery sidewalks, carefully looking both ways before crossing and steering far away from dogs. As we crossed the parking lot, I felt the black asphalt melt beneath my soles. Inside, the A&P had a clean linoleum floor. As the electric door slid open, a cool breeze blew through my face and hair; I gulped it down. Pheng stretched his arms to be picked up by one of my parents. He suddenly became shy and scared—a burden.

Food was everywhere. Stacks and stacks of cereal boxes. So much to choose from. I knew I couldn't take anything I wanted, so I let Mom and Dad select what we needed. I thought if I remained quiet, they might let me choose a piece of candy as a reward. We came to some asparagus, and Mom was about to start thumbing through the greenest bunch when suddenly Pheng had to pee.

My parents had only been in the United States for a year, so they couldn't speak English well yet. Frantically looking around, they concluded there weren't any restrooms in the store—after all, there weren't any restrooms at any of the stores in Laos. It would take us a good fifteen minutes to get home, much too long, and we needed groceries. If Dad took Pheng home, then Mom wouldn't know how to get back home. Looking around the vegetable aisles, Mom ripped off one of the plastic bags for packing vegetables in and told Pheng to go to the corner with her. Dad played the part of a partition and I was the lookout. Mom opened up the bag and Pheng urinated in it. Then she tied it real tight so it wouldn't leak.

"Oh, Nai, why don't you carry this?" Mom said, holding up the urine-filled plastic bag.

"No way!"

"Well, I don't see a garbage can around, so why don't you carry it until we get outside?"

"Why don't you make Pheng carry it? It's his urine," I protested.

"He's too little to carry it, and he might drop it."

"Nooo . . . why don't you or Dad carry it?" I was about to cry.

"Here, take it."

I slowly extended my hand, "I knew we shouldn't have brought Pheng with us."

"What was that you said? I didn't ask you to come." Mom glanced sideways at me.

The bag felt warm, and it looked like it had been filled with apple juice. I carried it carefully, afraid to let it get too near me, yet afraid to let it drop. People were gawking. I heard Mom laughing about how they were probably curious to know what was in the bag I was holding. I trudged slowly behind, thinking, now they'll have to buy me some candy, maybe some Hubba Bubba bubble gum.

Finally, we came to the cash register. By this time, Pheng's urine had gotten cold.

"Cash, check, or charge?" the young boy at the register asked.

"Yes," replied my father.

"Are you paying by cash, check, or charge?" he asked again.

"Yes," replied my father again.

The cashier decided to ring up all the groceries. My father handed him the cash, and I dashed outside. I couldn't see a single trash can around, so I carried Pheng's pee until we passed the parking lot. Then I tossed it with all my strength and the bag popped a few feet away.

When we returned home and unloaded all the groceries, there was a Tonka Truck for Pheng, but nothing for me.

Hmong Women

Mayli Vang

Who will refuse to die by the wayside
of cultural existence?

the woman who at thirteen
becomes the property of her mother's
thirty-five-year-old nephew
sold for a bar of silver and a feast of roosters

the woman who at twenty-one
is forked in the forearm for serving
burnt rice to her husband's mother
begging in the end for his forgiveness

the woman who at thirty-five
swallows her grief and hatred
holding her husband's fifteen-year-old bride
on the night of his matrimonial bliss

the woman who at forty-six
has given birth to a dozen children
washing their clothes every Tuesday morning
at the nearest Hi-Lake Laundromat
the woman who at seventy-three
still picks the tomatoes in Fresno, California
during the windless days of heated summers
dividing her income with her two sons

the old woman across the crowded street
with callused fingers eating sticky rice
in the basement of her children's home
where she sleeps on the cardboard box.

The Different Past

Open Hands and the Man with One Leg Shorter

Pos Moua

They liked to think they were not leaving their homes
after so many centuries of inhabiting those places.
They thought of themselves as going on an unsafe passage
and they thought they would come again
as other forms of living beings—when they no longer
lived in their present bodies—to the openness of the day,
to where the sun is high and the wind whistles in the field.

But it was hard for them
to be kind and gentle to those with open hands
waiting to be filled with rice; Open Hands, the sick
crying out for those who could no longer give;
Open Hands, signs of reaching out for a way
of arriving at the river that will connect to their wandering
spirits and restore the starving hearts.
Along the road they must go.

There were only a few who were sparing enough to have
a small bag or a scorched bamboo container of corn or rice.
Carrying one of the bags meant you were unlikely to be left behind.

The man with his wife and four children were the last group
in a long trail of people going away from their old places,
and he was carrying a roasted bamboo with rice ready to eat inside it.
A crippled man skipped to him and asked, "Elder brother,
will you give a palm of rice to last me another day? I am
not in good health to keep up with the rest of the group."
Everyone could see his eyes the moment he said that.

The man, thinking of his wife and children, knew
and replied, "I will not give, for I have four children to feed.
This isn't enough to last us through these woods."

After climbing a height and crossing a brook, they stopped
to look behind, to remember what was left behind:
That man with one leg shorter than the other, he might have
been the first to lead the rest. That man, with eyebrows lowered
after being turned down, looked away, and remained there forever.

Passing at the Canyon

Pos Moua

They were themselves passing, passing the man
with one leg shorter, as if he were just another
stone along their path. The man was simply himself
and the stone itself was ever more sad for the man.

Having seen so many passings, and their children wearied,
the feel of the daylight soothed them when the wind
coming from an open canyon blew on their tired faces.

To cross the canyon, without cutting around it
or without letting the soldiers discover them, they walked
on the fallen tree that bridged the two worlds.

Parents forbade their children
to look below or mention what was below.

Some children managed to glance
and saw what was a body, facedown, wearing brightly
colored clothes, like the traditional clothes their mothers wore.
But they did not know the meaning of these colors.
They were frightened of it, lying on sharp rocks below.
The sight of this passing left the children wondering
how many more passings were left to see.

The Old Man by the Road They Go

Pos Moua

That old man will not die of old age, but his death
under the wet tent, roofed by banana leaves,
chilled anyone passing by.

They passed by him pretending they didn't see him,
pretending there were no ants
walking in and out of his mouth,
taking and breaking his lonely breaths away.

On this mountain road,
they passed by him
afraid he would, half dead,
half alive, chase after them.

There were those who traveled without a bag of rice.
There were those who traveled with a begging bowl,
and there were those who traveled without looking
back at the old man, lying there
by the side of the road,
looking at not looking.

There were those who walked forward and backward
looking only for the moon
so they could rest, thinking of who's to leave behind;
and there were those who wore food in their bellies
having not a bit of compassion for the old man
who was trying to cry or speak with his innocent
but shadowed, half-awakened eyes.

This man, with his bones showing and
soft wrinkles covering his skin,
was trying to shine his spirit
to all those who passed by;
to those who looked to cross the river without death;
to those who feared ghosts and Pi-nyu-waih*
and all those who would not sing when they were left behind
with strangers—rocks, caves, or decaying tree trunks.

He will not die of old age, abandoned
underneath those green banana leaves.

---

*Tiny monkeylike forest creatures endowed with the power to bring sickness and
death to people.

The People beneath a Moon by the River

Pos Moua

After long months of wandering without knowing
how the river will unfold for them,
they're people beneath a moon before the river
preparing to settle for the night
and to pray to their ancestors for a safe crossing,
like a crossing over a bridge into the clouds.
They ask in their prayers that the river will be one
which the water will open up to the land and let them
pass without fear of the unknown dead.

Their journey is like a journey toward the sun;
often the way toward it is not the way back to the home
they long for or remember, nor will it be a way to return
to the days in which they could sleep quietly before smelling
the sacred and delicious first-harvested rice in the morning noon.
They know the way they have come will be a way of memories
etching deep into their minds and hearts, like the etching and
fading of sands.

Before they rest to watch the silence of the river
reflected above in the night sky, they tell tales
to quiet their children. They tell, as if there
were no war, the tale of a goddess who journeys
to the moon, searching for a pond in which her lover
was held captive. But the children grow weary
and soon fall asleep, before the story ends.

But of all these tales they have not forgotten to include
those who would shoot them for the silver bars
they wear around their waists. With some of these stories
told and heard, some of them might not be able to hear of
the tale about themselves meeting the river, for they did not know
if their ancestral spirits would take them across the river
by a bridge made by the river.

The Ritual before Crossing the River

Pos Moua

Out from another dense mosquito forest,
the river lay open before the people
who travel only by moonlight.

There, hearing the soft waves whispering
the sorrow of leaving behind their peasant life and
having lost so many—
they could see the distant torchlight
burning dimly on the other side.

Above, the moon was not the same moon
which had guided them in their existence
and reminded them of seasons to plant crops
or to bury their dead. It was a simple relief of
hunger and thirst. It was simply a full moon
to be seen in the cold, calm night
and the water was the water.

The running river is a vast river,
the dance between the spirit and the flesh,
a story about the many and the few.
Many had sailed on its fluttering surface;
some had survived while others disappeared.
They died on this river in order to return
to the spirit realm of the Nine Dragons
or to return to the place where
their spirits will take another life as flowers,
horses, birds, or human beings.

The people drank their first water from it.
In their legend, this river has two sources:
Those who want to know the meaning of life
must go to the one springing water, the beginning
of the Mekong—high in the mountains
of China—where there will be only disease.

And those who want life in bliss
or without suffering, must drink
to return to the second source.
There, they'll find the sweet sorrow
of wanting forever, and must never again return.

But to respect both sources, whether they drink
to return to the next life or not,
they cup water in the palms of their hands
and pour it on their heads and their children's,
touching the river with care because they have
not been touched by the flow of the water for months.
Then they rode in canoes secretly arranged for them,
gliding as if to hold close to the river,
straight toward the world where the torches are burning.

Reflected Light

Hilary Tham

We come into the world with a cry,
we protest
having to resume the burden of flesh.
We are recycled souls, Chinese elders say.
We return again and again to the Wheel, drink
the tea of Oblivion, forget we do not want
to dance the dance again.

Mother said she had been a man in a previous
life, a butcher with a bad temper
said the Book of Three Lives.

In Ampang Temple, a Taoist nun
showed me my present life
in the book. A pen-and-ink drawing
of a Manchu scholar asleep
over his books. Great potential,
great laziness, she said.
She told me I was the wife
of a corrupt official in my past
life, said my future life was still blank.

I did not ask about my dead sister,
her third life, if she had been reborn.
I was held by Mother's net of cautions:
Do not ask after the dead.
Words have power, names have power.
Speaking the names of the dead draws them
back to you. Let the dead go to their futures.

What I carry from that day in that temple,
is the aftertaste of a lie—the lie I spat out,
when she said I should atone for my past
with donations to the temple.

♦ ♦ ♦

Younger sister, death
stalked you,
took you when you were three.
Mother would not say your name
out loud. But last year she spoke your name.
A Taoist told her you died because she
gave you a killing name, a name that called to death.
She named you Plum Blossom, forgot that the sounds
Choy and Mui also meant "brittle" and "decay."

Zen teachers say, "Everything is Zen.
The silence of birds when a tiger walks by,
the deer catching tiger scent,
the click of tiger teeth meeting in deer's throat,
the absence of hunger as tiger feeds, are Zen
and not Zen. Zen is Nothingness."
The student stares and longs for certainties, home.

Home is a place, with real things—hot rice,
beds to sleep in, shoes we remove
beside the front door to enter the house.
It is a place in the mind
where people were less kind than
we remember. Or kinder.
Memory is an erratic camera, with
variable film and faulty zoom button.
Memory is a telescope we view from both ends.

What I hold in my memory is a truth of you,
the three-year-old I knew, a cameo from the past,
withdrawn from time's revisions.
You wear, forever, rounded lips, soft hair,
wide eyes unchanged.
This is not the truth. Your truth was a stream
seeping through soil, around rocks, spreading,
reaching the thirst of trees and grass.

♦ ♦ ♦

Teenagers are as misunderstood as tadpoles.
At thirteen, I wanted
to believe I was adopted,
to believe I could disown the family,
their voices and their needs.
I dreamed of a room of my own.

One night I stood in the dark and
thought about leaving home.
I stared until I was dizzy, gazing at stars.
I was nothing to them, not even a flicker
of a shadow on a leaf.
Somewhere a dog barked. And fell silent.
Only a frog in the weeds refused silence,
plaintively calling for a mate. A second frog
answered. And another. Soon the weeds were filled
with the multitudinous presence of frogs.

My mother had a story about the creation of frogs:
how a poor couple was buried alive in a mud slide.
A passing god heard their muffled calling—
"On," "Long": "Husband," "Wife,"
even as mud filled their ears, their mouths.
He gifted them with amphibian life,
changed them into frogs.

I listened to the frogs, their voices
telling a sad tale of mud, calling
to be heard, wanting to know someone
they loved was still there to love them.
Then I went in to my family

♦ ♦ ♦

The first time I saw ronggeng—
the traditional dance of the Malays—
I wanted to stand and watch forever.

Ronggeng couples move as one,
their timing perfectly matched,
feet linked by invisible strings,
one stepping forward as the other
steps back, one advancing
as the other retreats,
almost touching, always keeping
a weave of air between, never touching.
How well the dancers ronggeng
depends
on how close to each
other they can come
without touching.

The words of the song tease:
"Rasa Sayang—The feel of love . . ."

◆ ◆ ◆

When I was twenty, I said,
All men are false,
their minds like sparrows,
feet hot on electric wires against sky.
They take off and go when the wind blows
long hair, young life.

At thirteen, I despised the unequal,
struggling marriages in my hometown, envied
the serenity of the nuns at school.
I wanted to be a nun.

At sixteen, I had learned Te, Virtue,
too well to abandon my parents as
they aged. Sitting on a curve of rain tree
root, I broke open seed pods, dry with ripeness,
picked out the red seeds. Threw them one by one
into the drain. They stayed where they landed.
No water flowed in the drain.

I remember the dry feel of dust
between my toes, and the light leaving
the sky, the road; the road that ran forever
to where land touched sky. I remember
the crows overhead squawking, bidding
others settle down, quit rocking the branch.

Love is messy, life is messy, I told myself.
The product of love is life. The product
of life is love. Love which does not last.
Babies are delivered in a puddle of blood
and water. When we die, we leave our bodies
leaking for worms. I thought of hospitals
and delivery rooms and postal systems
and said: We are God's mailing system; each birth
is a solicitation: "Please contribute . . ."

◆ ◆ ◆

The world is a hard place—
it began with stone
pillars on a turtle's back*
and ends in stone
chiseled with our names;
Between the making
and the unmaking, flesh
and blood, bone and hair,
and then we; they are not there.
We look at our empty hands
and feel shadows and shade,
skin drying where water has been,
and are left with wind, know them
only by their absence. Water. Wind.

*In Chinese mythology, four stone pillars hold up Heaven.

The Driver Conrado's Penitent Life

Eugene Gloria

The scent of food was everywhere he turned,
the vendor stirring his flat black pan,
the scalding oil for the glazed plantains
and the afternoon darkening like the toll of bells
announcing: time to eat, time to go.
But the driver Conrado was steady
with each pop of the Chiclets he chewed,
a pocket of air would balloon in his mouth,
while the boy fidgeted with the radio knob
for some new song his sisters sang.
Conrado, this piece-packing ex-military,
lackey of a petty bureaucrat, Conrado
whose stern eyebrows could answer
yes better than his mouth, Conrado
who almost served time if not for *Sir,*
waits, patient as a sniper.
Beyond the driver was the moon
and below its fat face stood the school
where inside the bureaucrat was moonlighting
in front of rows of desks, his fingers dusted
with chalk and his mouth drying with words.
What he said to his pupils was difficult
and dull as the distant planets, while the moon
hung brighter than the vendor's lamp.
When the boy's father emerged from the school,
the world turned slightly. Night
became this father of secrets
and all the hard science the boy hungered to master.
The father slumped his wide shoulders forward,
declared to his driver with the authority
that his own class enjoined: *Time to go*
Conrado, the boy is hungry, it's time we go.

Tilting the Continent

The Family with Three Madonnas

Oliver de la Paz

The first Madonna's languid arm gleams from television light. Tired in her blue robe she sees on-screen lovers kiss, like the snooze of boats drifting past. Through the snow of the cathode, snores of a man on the sofa, alone. It is raining and the roar of the tube turned furnace makes the Madonna dream. Outside, the porch light kills the sky while birches burn with fireflies trembling through a storm.

◆ ◆ ◆

The second Madonna, stern on the dash of the car, lifts her eyes to the rearview mirror when Maria Elena puts it in reverse. She stands, hands folded like a mast, and frowns at the cars in repose. Some of the drivers stare straight ahead, listening to invisible trees. Look there, through the windshield—the cry of a disintegrating star.

◆ ◆ ◆

The third Madonna holds cracks in her porcelain hands. She rests in the closet next to a pair of sneakers. There are reasonable coats hung like perfect gentleman. They spill into the dark, strangers . . . like the one just stepped off a train wearing a white camellia in his lapel. Through the glass as the train steams by damp houses, a woman with a blue hat dreams in roses.

The Healing

Lan Duong

Sister 2 is sick. She says,
"Lan, do it for me good now. I feel
so tired."
Her nurse's hands withdraw the yellowed bra
and her small breasts
dipped into a mother's sadness
flatten into the mattress.

I straddle her waist,
my strong legs
lie weak
next to hers.

Her tough flesh is hammered brown
by father's furies
and sprays of hot acne
trickle down her back.
Because ma ate too much ot,
it's in our blood,
she always laughs soft.

I rain eucalyptus oil
in burning green puddles
in the trenches
of her back
bowed
to the ancients of ours
to the father, the brother, and the husband.

I rake the edge of a quarter
down the ridges of spine
past the tattoo of scars
Hard and harder still. Until.
her skin spits a red skeleton
from the silver agitations. And long after
she falls asleep. Long after
she draws a deep breath
and the blood is released,
the coin feels cool green
between my fingers
and the smell
rides
in my hair
for days.

Hilo

LeAna B. Gloor

Oh Mother, I think you would like it here,
all the Filipinos have smile lines
and pretend they aren't poor.
How I love their wrinkled faces,
I smile and buy their bitter melon
gladly,
and they are never sure why I smile at them so long,
why I touch their hands as the coins are passed.
I bathe in their soft Tagalog,
their voices wash away the loneliness
a bit.

Oh Mother, I think you would like it here,
these are the uncles and aunties
you left behind,
here in the Hilo farmers' market
they've been waiting for you,
each harvest
they've been reaping your old tears into fruit,
like home, Momma,
like home.

Mole on My Foot

Aurora Harris

Eight-thirty A.M. Houston, Texas time
Where El Niño's tears have fallen
For the past three hours
Where the first bird sings
Between dripping and splashes—
Rain rolling off frayed banana leaves—
Where outside this room
Is the outside of Quezon City
The outside that surrounded
The house on Banahaw Street
Where my pet lizards and Japanese snails
Gathered in the garden
Where six a.m. humidity was the scent of
Tinapay, yeasty rolls, sold in buttered
Brown paper bags when I bought cans of
condensed milk—Asian baby on the label
From a shack on a dirt road that dusted my feet—

Where inside this room
This city called Houston
Is filled with the sweetness of sandalwood oil,
Tranquillity oil and apricot scrub for tired skin
Where the Black and Asian/Pacific Island me
Was easily received by
El Mundo's Cabeza
That came in the shapes of
Vietnamese and Jews
African Americans and
Hispanics
Native Americans and
Caucasians
Poets and writers from
Michigan Montana Texas California
And Women and Women and Women
With Women—

I take my right foot
Slippery with oil
And slide it on my thigh.
I take my right foot
And take a long look
Because Poet Long Chu said,
A mole on a foot means
You are meant to travel—

And there is one there!
Small dark brown mole
One inch below
My baby toe
And another one is forming.

I wonder if this means
The start of new travels
While a plane's rumble
Fills light gray skies.

I wonder if this means
The start of new travels
While morning bird returns
To harmonize with the rain.

I wonder if this means
The start of new travels
While rain becomes pearls
To be swallowed by azaleas
In a Jungian dream *el*
color de azujelo. *

---

* *Azujelo* (Spanish)—a brightly colored tile of the Near East, Spain, and Holland.

Infected

Marianne Villanueva

It was a disease, their stepmother said. The children came back from Manila, and suddenly they stopped listening to her. They were running around the apartment, infected with restlessness. "Pick up your shoes . . . pick up your clothes," she would tell them. Their father yelled at them. He was a tall, imposing man with a large nose. His glasses slid down and made him look like a strange type of bird.

The eldest, a girl, almost nine, looked at him and thought how strange her father looked standing there, hands clenched. She thought, He doesn't understand. All she wanted were Polly Pockets. Back home in her room in Manila, there were Polly Pockets lined up in rows on shelves that her grandmother had put up for her in her mother's old room. There was also a dollhouse, with a rug that her now-dead mother had made for the miniature living room. There, the girl had her own four-poster canopied bed and white sheets with eyelet ruffles. The girl would bounce up and down on the bed. Stretched out, looking at the white pillows against the dark wood of the bedposts, she could almost think she was a queen.

In New York, where the children lived, it was starting to get cold. They stood on the street corner, waiting for the school bus, pressed against each other for warmth. The wind blew down the avenue, making their cheeks red. They held each other's hands. When the school bus came, they told each other, "Hurry up, hurry up!" They clutched their heavy school satchels. They struggled onto the bus in their bulky coats, their heavy lace-up shoes.

When they got home, their father was angry. Pick up your shoes, he would say over and over. They didn't understand what the thing was about the shoes. The shoes seemed to materialize in the living room, in the hallway, in spite of themselves. Then they would go scurrying around, scooping up the hateful things, the things with the laces that were so hard to tie in the mornings, that always got their fingers in knots just when they needed to be out the door.

The food was different, too. After a summer of eating rice cakes, they didn't want to go back to eating frozen chicken nuggets and fish sticks, which was all the two maids served them because their father and stepmother both worked in a bank and kept late hours, and the maids were lazy when the master and mistress were not at home. It was not just the rice cakes the children missed, but the vegetables boiled in coconut milk, and the garlicky taste of the chicken. Their tongues curled backward when they looked at the frozen food heated up in the microwave. Their stomachs, distended and full from a diet rich in pork and rice, suddenly seemed to shrivel up and sometimes the New York food would not go down and came back up the wrong way and then the stepmother flew into a passion. "I have to be at work," she would say. "Do you understand? I have a job! I have to be at work!"

So finally their father threatened them. "I will never send you back there again," he said. He was English and his parents were always telling him how spoiled his children were. For a week, the children were quiet. The two eldest talked about it and decided they must tiptoe around the apartment, especially when their stepmother was reading.

One evening, their grandmother called from Manila. Their father would not let them talk to her, but they knew it was their grandmother. Their father kept them out of the room and spoke in low, hushed tones. They pressed their ears against the bedroom door, listening. They could imagine their father's head moving up and down, up and down as he talked. That stentorian voice. They liked listening to their grandmother, the way her voice moved up and down, like a pianist practicing scales. She must have been talking about Christmas plans. When they were in Manila for the summer, their grandmother had told them they would be visiting her again at Christmas. But now their father came out of his bedroom and said they were not going to Manila for Christmas; they were going to Mexico. Mexico! Did they know anyone in Mexico? "No," their father said. "We will stay in a hotel. It will be warm there. We will stay on a beach. Your stepmother needs to relax. This has all been a great strain on her."

The girl grew wild with disappointment. She thought of her aunt, her mother's sister, in San Francisco. She had the telephone number, written down somewhere. Where was it? She searched frantically in all her coat pockets. Her aunt had called one day, when her father was out. She had made the girl write down the number, saying it slowly and carefully, so that the girl could write it down in her laborious script. "Now remember," the aunt had said, "you must always dial one when it's long distance. Remember, always begin with the one." Her aunt spoke deliberately and slowly, as though it was very, very important that the girl understand this.

◆ ◆ ◆

The girl understood what her aunt was trying to say. Her aunt was worried. The new mother was very thin and had never had children. She was forty-two, four years older than their father. She was always impatient, complaining whenever the children, scurrying around her, accidentally jostled her or trod on the toes of her high-heeled shoes. She acted as though she were being buffeted by a high wind. "Do not come near me!" she would yell. "Keep away!"

Now where was her aunt's number? Because the girl was always forgetting where she put things, and her room was always cluttered with toys that the maids then tossed haphazardly into the corners when it was time to vacuum, this number had vanished and the girl never found it.

The middle boy was always having accidents. He dropped things. He didn't dare tell his father that in Manila, his grandmother rubbed his body with hot oil every night before going to bed. It was the ritual he enjoyed the most. His grandmother rubbed his body, stretched out naked on the cool sheets, and slowly his mind would drift. Very soon, he was asleep. In New York, there was no one to rub his body. He hugged feather pillows. They were too soft and did not feel like the hands of his grandmother. His body sank into them; they were unresisting, inert things. He had nightmares. In the middle of the night, he would cry out. "Jesus Christ!" his father would yell. "Jesus Christ!"

The youngest was five. He looked the most like his mother. He had her eyes and her splayed toes. This, at least, was what everyone in Manila told him. He remembered very little about his mother, but he knew he looked like her. There were no pictures of her in the apartment anymore, so when he tried to think about his mother, he looked in the mirror. She must have been light-skinned, then, and had a small mouth. The aunt in San Francisco had a mouth with thick, full lips. They had spent a few days with her in the spring. She was always hugging and kissing. "Does your new mother do this?"

she asked the little boy once. "No," he said. "Why not?" the aunt said. "I don't know," the child said.

And after that, back in New York, he would observe other mothers with their children: how they held their children's hands; how concern seemed to jump into their faces whenever they shepherded their children across the street. But I have a mother, he would think.

Before the new mother came, they only had their father. But they had all of him. He would come home from the office, loosen his tie, and, still in his suit, get down on all fours in the playroom. The children would scream with delight. They would hang on to his neck, his shoulders. He didn't care if they pulled at his glasses, or rumpled his clothes. His shoes were all scuffed. But this was their father before. Now that he had married again, he had forgotten how to get down on all fours. Now he was always telling them to behave. At dinnertime, which when their parents were home was a formal meal at which the children had to sit very quietly on the stiff-backed chairs and wait until it was their turn to be served, he seemed weary. The stepmother had a nervous way of looking around. Craning her head this way and that, she would say, "Where's the salt? . . . What happened to the butter dish?" This would send ripples of nervousness through the children. Was the salt under the table? Did one of them put it there? They couldn't remember. Where was the butter dish? What did it look like? Had they even seen it at all? They would look at her, jumpy in their seats. Their stepmother was exasperated. Dinner never went as planned. There was always something going wrong. The children could not behave. Either their elbows would fly out while they were spooning food onto their plates, or something would drop to the floor. Their stepmother would roll her eyes, and their father's face would grow red with embarrassment. "Don't you know how to eat?" he would say. Sometimes he would send them away. "Go to your room," he would say. They jumped up then, feeling a great surge of excitement and joy. But they must not run. They knew this. They tried to walk slowly, carefully, putting one foot in front of the other, until they were all the way down the hallway and into their own section of the apartment. They would fling themselves on their beds. Without talking, they all began thinking of the same thing: the house in Manila, surrounded by mango trees; the swimming pool with its clear blue water; the black dog in the kitchen; the lovebirds in cages; the smells.

The middle child would get up and start playing with his Sega games. *Pow! Pow! Pow!* He had Mortal Kombat II. He was Subzero. He was Reptile. He could send snakes shooting out of the palms of his hands. Get down here! The words "Flawless Victory" imprinted on his brain and obliterated the shards of memory.

After a while, the eldest, too, would get up. But she was very listless. She would take up her Barbie dolls, one after the other. They all looked the same: all platinum blond, with long hair. None of them looked like her. She was dark. Her skin, her hair, and her eyes were dark. People in Manila said she looked like her grandmother. She didn't know what to play with. She wandered aimlessly around the room, touching this and that.

The youngest lay on his bed, sucking his thumb and looking at the ceiling. He hadn't told the others, but once, in a park by the East River, he had seen his old nanny, the one who had been with them when their mother was still alive. At least, he had thought it was her, though when she saw him, and he smiled and waved, she didn't respond. She was pushing a blond little boy in a stroller. The nanny was from the Philippines, like the children's mother, and for two years after their mother died, and before their father married again, she had taken care of them. But the stepmother did not like her because, she said, the nanny "talked back." So she had sent the nanny away.

The youngest had stared at the nanny, but she was already turning her back. He wanted to bawl, but he was afraid of what his sister would say. The nursemaid did not look in his direction again. Now he turned his head to the pillow. He would suck his thumb all evening.

Once a week, the stepmother took them to a doctor. Only, this doctor just wanted to talk. She was a thin, middle-aged woman with graying hair. The three of them sat in front of her, looking down at their shoes. When she could not get them to talk, she gave them paper and crayons. "Draw me a picture," she told them. The girl drew pictures of women in kimonos. "Is that your mother?" the doctor asked. "No," the girl said. "I just like looking at women in kimonos."

The middle child drew pictures of airplanes and people falling down and cracking their heads on cliffs. The doctor would ask to speak to the father privately. "This is very disturbing," the doctor said. She took the pictures and showed them to the boy's father. "Your child is disturbed," she said.

The youngest drew nothing at all. If pushed, he would draw a square. Just an empty square, nothing else. Children like to draw, the doctor would tell him. He would shrug, let the crayon slip from between his fingers.

The girl's old piano teacher had moved away while they were in Manila. Now there was a new teacher: Russian, with steel-gray hair and wire-rimmed glasses. The girl found it difficult to understand her. Sometimes the teacher would become exasperated and after many times telling the girl to put her fingers on a particular key, she would reach out with her gnarled fingers, making the girl start and shrink backward. The woman's fingers were hard from years of pounding the ivory keys. The girl was not interested in the piano. When her father heard her slow, hesitant practicing on the piano in the living room, it made him grit his teeth. He did not like to be reminded of his first wife, to whom the piano belonged. The piano had belonged to his first wife's mother for many years, and then she had it shipped to New York. His first wife loved to play Beethoven sonatas.

When Halloween came, the girl said she wanted to be Ginger Spice. She wanted a Ginger Spice jacket: short and tight, with a Union Jack motif. Then, when it came close to Halloween, she suddenly changed her mind and said she wanted to be Baby Spice, the pretty blond one. She wanted the blond pigtails and the short skirt and the spaghetti-strap top. To her surprise, the stepmother became very solicitous and immediately ordered up an outfit from a dressmaker, even taking the girl in for fittings after school. The middle boy said he wanted to be the stalker in *Scream*—the one who dresses in black and wears the mask. The father did not know anything about *Scream*, but there was a big toy store around the corner from their apartment. This toy store was on Eighty-seventh Street, and one weekend he took the boy there and they selected a costume that looked just like the one worn by the character in the movie: the white rubber mask with the trailing black hole for a mouth, and the black robe. The youngest child said he did not want to be anything. The stepmother lost her patience and called him "naughty." He spent a lot of time looking out the big plate glass windows of their ninth-floor apartment, down at the street below. Whenever anyone asked what he was doing there, he would say he was counting yellow cabs.

Actually, he thought he had once seen the edge of his mother's cream bathrobe. The edge of it drifted out in the air, but she herself was around the corner of the building and he couldn't see her. "Come and see!" he'd cried out to his older sister, tugging her by the hand. When she'd come and looked, she said only, "That's the smoke from the roof of the next building." There was always some sort of smoke drifting by, from manholes on the street—something cooking down there, the boy would wonder?—or from the roofs of adjacent buildings. But the boy was sure that his mother was drifting outside the window. She's come for me, he thought to himself. And afterward, he was always by the window. The smoke that drifted by sometimes seemed to him to have a peculiar shape, like that of a woman peering in the windows. At these times he could not say exactly that it reminded him of his mother, but he was always watching and waiting for her.

Once he overheard an argument between his stepmother and his father. They were arguing about him, about why he liked staying by the window so much.

"It's that woman," his stepmother was saying, and the boy knew she was talking about his old nanny. "Came here the other day . . . just dropped by," she said. "Taking her new charge out for a stroll . . . he lives somewhere on Ninetieth. They just happened to be passing by the building. She tells him things."

After that, the father said he would have a talk with the nanny. He would tell her she must not stop by anymore. It was bad for the children.

Early in the afternoon of Halloween, the aunt from San Francisco called. "Are you going trick-or-treating?" she wanted to know. "What are you going to be?" The two older children were very excited, describing their costumes to her. The youngest would not speak, and so the oldest girl said, "He's going to be a dog! He's going to follow me around on all fours, like a puppy!" This made the aunt laugh. She had no idea whether the girl was joking or serious. They told her that Regis Philbin, the talk show host, lived in their building, and that every Halloween he gave out huge parcels of candy. So they would be sure to ring the bell of his apartment. And there were a few other people in the building who gave a lot of candy, but most of the people were old women with harshly painted mouths and strings of pearls, who cared nothing for children holding out bags and asking for candy.

But the youngest child is distracted and doesn't think about Halloween. He sees his mother hovering outside the plate glass window in a blue housedress decorated with tiny pink flowers. At least, he knows it is his mother, though her face is obscured by a shimmering whiteness. She stretches out her arms to him. He goes to the window, and he looks down, and her feet are standing on air. Now she stretches out both arms to him. Below him, the traffic on Park Avenue is snarled. A cab has tried to make a right turn from the wrong lane and now cars are beeping. But the noise is very far away. His mother is speaking to him. She says, over and over, "Not too good . . . not too good," and the child knows she is speaking about him. Because last night his stepmother spanked him. He had broken something, he can't now remember what. But it was in his stepmother's room, and it was precious to her. He knew it was precious only after it was broken. When the thing lay in shards on the carpet. Then his stepmother wailed. She called him a demon. She said there was something inside him, something bad, that made him do these things. His older brother and sister only looked on, frightened, when the stepmother was carrying on.

His father came. He was very angry and dragged the youngest child to his room. The youngest child stayed there all evening, sobbing.

One day, the youngest child was about to go out. He stood in the foyer, waiting for the elevator. Then he saw her, his old nanny. She seemed to have been waiting for some time. With her was a blond child in a stroller. The youngest child looked in fascination at this other being, and remarked how its mouth seemed to form little O's at intervals, as though yearning to suck. The nanny hugged him to her. "You're so thin!" she kept saying, over and over. She brushed his hair out of his eyes. She asked after the other two children. "They're in their room, watching TV," said the youngest child. He was alone in the foyer with his old nanny, and it seemed his heart must burst from happiness.

They heard a noise. The woman gave a start. "I have to go," she said, trying to free her skirt from the youngest child's fingers. "No! No!" he cried. He buried his face between her legs. He thought he could smell damp earth there and he liked it. But she pushed him away. "If your father asks, you know what to say," she told him.

She hurried down the corridor to the elevator. Now the youngest child wandered to the window. Again he saw his mother there. Only now her face was distinct. He saw it clearly: the dark eyes, the full cheeks. Every feature of her face was as clear as a photograph. And she was looking at him with her arms outstretched.

He looked down at the avenue. The yellow cabs were there honking, but the sound seemed again to be coming from a great distance. The boy would have climbed onto the window ledge, but his mother shook her head and mouthed the word "No." Her voice was gentle. He thought she looked sad.

Then the boy's sister came running out, looking for him. She saw him at the window and asked him what he was looking at. But the youngest child looked at his mother, and she had a finger raised to her lips, so he did not reply. Instead, he pointed at the busy cabs on the avenue. The girl said, "You are a funny boy," and ran away again. The youngest child saw his mother looking longingly after her.

The youngest child saw that his mother was wearing flowered cloth slippers. These he had seen in a box in the hall closet once. He went to the hall closet now. He rummaged among the boxes, but though he opened box after box, the one with the cloth slippers had disappeared.

One of the maids came out of the kitchen. "Bad boy!" she told him. "Look what a mess you've made! I will tell your father when he gets home!"

He looked again at his mother in the window. She only shook her head sadly at him and smiled.

Now the youngest child spent all his time at the window. "What are you doing?" the stepmother said impatiently. "Get away from there!" She was afraid he might fall out. She knew of the terrible mishap involving Eric Clapton's child. The maids were under strict orders to keep the boy away from the window.

But the maids were too busy to keep an eye on him all day. They were both from the Philippines and loved to talk to each other in the kitchen. There were long stretches of the day when they forgot about the youngest child. Left to himself, he always went to the window. His mother was always there now, waiting for him. She always brightened up when he came.

Once the boy tried to tell his sister what he was seeing. He asked his sister if she remembered her mother, and she said, "Of course!"

He asked her what their mother had looked like, and his sister said, "She had black hair." He asked his sister if she would know their mother if their mother were to appear again. His sister gave him a strange look. "I would know her. Of course I would know her," she said. But no matter how often his sister passes the window, she never turns her head, even when her mother is staring straight at her. And this is how the youngest child knows he is the only one who can see his mother, his mother who waits by the window and looks in.

In November it began to snow. It snowed so hard that all the schools were closed for a few days. Then all the children were home, and the maids complained about how tired they were, picking up after them all day long. The stepmother was sick in bed with a cold. She never left her room.

The youngest child found that it was hard for him to see his mother sometimes, in the whirling snow. Her face was obscured by a strange whiteness. One evening, when his father was reading a newspaper in the living room, the youngest child saw his mother pass through the window glass—a white shape, more like mist than anything else—and come up to his father as he sat in his old armchair. She stood there for a few moments, and the youngest child held his breath. But his father merely scratched his nose and continued reading. Then his mother, who was now an indistinct white shape, began to make a slow circuit of the room. She stopped before the piano. The lid was open and it seemed to the boy that the keys trembled, but they made no sound. Then she moved in front of a painting of his stepmother. It had been painted when the stepmother was only nineteen. She was very beautiful, with rich, flowing black hair and large, sparkling eyes. His mother seemed to shudder. At once her light refracted into many shimmering crystals. These hung in the air briefly and disappeared.

The middle child's nightmares grew worse. Once or twice the maids heard him call out "Paz," which was his dead mother's name. The maids whispered and crossed themselves. The stepmother became frantic. She said the apartment had been visited by evil spirits. One of her secretaries at work told her about exorcisms, and she had her husband call a priest. The priest walked around the rooms, swinging a censer and intoning a blessing. The youngest child saw his mother watching from the window. She was smiling.

Then the stepmother insisted that they must sell the apartment. "The hall is too short," she said. She wanted a better view. The father talked to a number of real estate agents. The children looked around them at the familiar rooms and did not know what to do.

The eldest collected her dolls and told them they would soon be going to a new place. She imagined that in the new place, the children's rooms would be as far away as possible from their father's room. "Then we'll hardly see him," she whispered to her favorite Barbie, the one who was dressed like Princess Jasmine in *Aladdin*.

The middle child took to lurking in the kitchen with the maids. They reminded him of his grandmother, with their strange talk, though the maids had lived in New York for so long that they remembered little about their home villages and would never go back there even if they could afford to. When the middle child slid onto a high stool and leaned his elbows on the kitchen counter, the maids only looked at him and laughed. They were not cruel, but the father was too busy, the stepmother too cold. They had heard of a grandmother in the Philippines, an aunt in San Francisco, but these relatives never came. The maids had the apartment to themselves most of the time. Their friends were envious because they had so much freedom. But the maids themselves were not happy. They grumbled that the master didn't pay them enough to stay in a haunted apartment, with three such unlikable children. So why pay attention to the boy? Let him sit there! They continued to chatter with each other.

The grandmother called again from the Philippines. It seemed to the children, listening from behind a closed door, that their father and their grandmother were having an argument. It seemed the grandmother didn't want the children to go to Mexico for Christmas. She seemed to be reminding their father of a promise of some sort. They heard their father say, "It's very hard. Don't press me . . . don't press me." This was followed by a long silence. When their father came out of the bedroom, he had his lips tightly pressed together.

And then one day the youngest child no longer saw his mother at the window. He stared and stared, but she was gone. The smoke was only smoke, drifting lazily by. He wondered if the old priest who had come and said the prayers, who had filled the rooms with the bad-smelling odor of incense, had anything to do with his mother's disappearance. He went again and again to the window.

Yes, his mother was really gone.

He looked up at the gray sky between the tall buildings. He listened to the sound of traffic. He never again saw his mother's face, or watched her come through the glass as a white shadow.

The apartment on Park Avenue was sold after Christmas. Eventually the children grew up. The two oldest were sent to boarding school in England, as the father had planned. England is a cold country, even in summer. The children never stopped dreaming about the Philippines, the warm beaches, the swaying palm trees. But they were only allowed to see their grandmother every other year. She had grown old and stooped. Her hands were gnarled, and it hurt her fingers to straighten them. It seemed to the children that each time they saw their grandmother, a gray circle around the pupils of her eyes had grown larger. A hump seemed to be growing out of the middle of her back. She walked with a cane. She still sighed and said, "If only your mother had lived, how proud she would be . . ."

The girl went to college at Smith. She said she wanted to be a writer. The middle child drifted into college, though his grades were not quite as good as his sister's, and so he did not make it into an Ivy League school.

The stepmother said they were spoiled. She was still beautiful, her hair still the rich black it had been when the children first met her.

The youngest child was killed in a car accident the year after the apartment on Park Avenue was sold. It was very strange. He was crossing the avenue to go home from school. People said there were no cars coming from either direction when he left the sidewalk. And he *had* looked, contrary to what a child of that age might have been expected to do. Suddenly a black jeep had appeared, seemingly out of nowhere. The boy was flung up in the air and landed on the jeep's hood. There was a sickening thud, and when he landed on the pavement, his head bloody, the bystanders saw his arms and legs were already purple and starting to swell up.

His old nanny came to the hospital to visit him. He was not conscious, but perhaps he felt her tears. They fell on his inert hands and sprinkled the white hospital sheet. She crossed herself over and over, and people who happened to be nearby said she was commending the boy's soul to his mother's care.

Rio Grande

U Sam Oeur

For Rose and Wayne Rutherford

Sunday afternoon, the family I'm visiting
enters the sanctum of happiness, while I sit
in the shade on the bank of the Rio Grande
contemplating the water's tireless flow.

The water is transparent; I can see the rocks
in the riverbed. I feel content in the company
of this river whose source I do not know.
Its banks are decorated with colorful stones.

As I observe the walls of the gorge
I see beautiful castles. Beyond my vision
stand the ruins of Bayon.* In front of me,
my friends float side by side in inner tubes.

The feelings of joy and satisfaction which
prevail in their hearts can be seen on their faces.
They are content with heaven and earth. Their hearts
unify like raindrops which have fallen into a bucket.

They float their inner tubes downstream, smiling.
They both wave their right hands at me
as they pass in front of me, then disappear
around the bend into paradise.

---

*Bayon: a temple city north of Angkor Wat, but still part of Angkor City. It was built circa A.D. 1200, while Angkor Wat was built from A.D 1113 to 1150.

I sneak a look up into space wondering how it is
that God has brought me to Taos to share their happiness.
Then here they are, returning by foot, blessed,
as if they have been bathed in Amrita!*

Translated by Ken McCullough

---

*Amrita (Sanskrit): the nectar of bliss.

Land of the Big Fruit

Toni Mesina

Mango season on Pauoa Road was a give-and-take relationship. The blossoms gave us sneezes, and we took the mangoes when those blossoms grew. Walking up the dead end, we saw a mango tree in what seemed to be every other front yard. Mom and Dad never planted a tree in our yard because our sensitive little noses couldn't take the irritation. Besides, with all the trees on the street, we already had enough fruit, and sneezes, than we needed.

One day, Mama-san called us over to help with the picking. Backpacks and all, Jessie, Jordan, and I ran over and fought over the remaining pole with the white bag at the top. Jessie and Jordan soon realized that together they maneuvered the bag around the mango better than they could alone. Because I was older, a little bigger, and a boy, Mama-san always let me struggle on my own.

"Jaime-chan, you come hee-ya. You biggah. Can liff dis one all by youself." She handed me the wooden pole and backed away. Getting the pole up was no problem. It was getting the mango down that I never understood, but the three of us didn't mind. Getting the mango in the bag was a feat for kids. Mama-san's husband, Old Koto, appeared from behind after we celebrated our haul for a minute and, as if by magic, an orange, greenish, yellow softball-sized fruit was sitting in his hands. Paper grocery bags full of mangoes quickly replaced the books in our backpacks and we headed home to show Dad our harvest.

"Dad! Dad!"

"Are your feet clean?" Dad asked from his post in the kitchen doorway at the top of the stairs. This question came out in a stern voice, but as we looked up, he smiled and ruffled our hair. "What did you do?" he asked, eyeing our bulging bags. "Take all the fruit off Mama-san's tree?" We stood around the table, gingerly opening our bags to reveal our treasures. Jordan always wanted to show off his kindergarten counting skills, and on this day, he counted fifteen. There were actually only thirteen because he skipped eight and twelve, but it was still a whole lot of fruit.

"Dad!" Jessie, my younger sister by two years, shouted as she pushed the long bangs from her face. "Me and Jordan—"

"Jordan and *I*," Dad corrected.

"Oh, yeah. Jordan and I wen pick da biggess one, even bigger dan da one Jaime wen pick!"

"Not!" I barked back. "Mines was bigger. An too, I wen ketch um all by myself."

"I wen count wrong. Only get fourteen mangoes," Jordan said, correcting himself as he played with the sap of a green mango the size of a baseball.

"You're gonna get itchy, son," Dad scolded as he took the fruit and put them in the sink for a good washing. "This is gonna taste so good with the bagoong. Grandma's gonna like this one." He sniffed the green mango before holding it under the water spout.

Grandma must have smelled the mangoes as soon as we walked in the door, because she was already in the kitchen reaching for a knife and a bowl, ready to peel. I grabbed the biggest mango that we brought home, the softball.

"Look, Grandma! Look! This one is sooooo big!" I was proud of my first mango of the season.

"Big? *Humph!*" she snorted. "You tink dass big? You should see de ones we hab in the Pilippines. Oh, dey are so big, as big as your head!" She softly knocked my forehead with her knuckles.

A mango as big as my head? No way! I thought. Dad turned to us and smiled. Maybe he knew Grandma was just pulling my leg.

Grandma pulled my leg every time I brought a huge fruit home. Later that year, I brought home a large guava. She said, "In Pasuquin, we hab guabas as big as de waterrrmelons here." In my nine-year-old, wisecracky way, I asked how big their watermelons were there. "Oh, as big as two waterrrmelons here."

"Dad?" I asked one afternoon as we were driving home from basketball practice, passing all the mango trees.

He was humming an Earth, Wind, and Fire song playing on the radio. "Yeah, son?"

"How come Grandma always says the mangoes are small? They hardly fit in two of my hands!" I held both my mitts up for him to see.

"Well," Dad began turning down the radio, "where Grandma grew up, the land is different. You know how the dirt is red by Auntie May's house in Pearl City and how it's brown here?"

"So what color is da dirt in 'de Pilippines?'" I imitated Grandma's accent.

158

"Maybe red, maybe brown, maybe purple. Who knows?" He shrugged.

"You ever been there, Dad?"

"To the Philippines?" He looked over at me and nodded. "Well, Grandma and Grandpa took me there when I was five years old, and I hardly remember anything. I went again when I graduated from high school, but didn't go to the countryside. I just stayed in Manila with my auntie Rose." He parked the car on the street because he was cleaning out the garage and everything was everywhere. "Don't forget your towel and ball in the back," he reminded as he nodded toward the backseat.

"So you don't remember where Grandma grew up? Never saw da huge trees wid da huge fruit?" I shut the car door.

"Nope, but I did see the big fruits at the market."

Wow! A country where the fruit was huge, bigger than Jordan's head. I couldn't imagine it. All this time I thought Grandma was exaggerating, but if Dad saw the fruit, who was I to doubt? I was just this little kid in Hawaii who knew nothing about "de Pilippines." It was this fantasyland where Grandma came from, and from where she got the most awesome stories.

I got *the* story a few years later.

When the three of us got a little older, Grandma had a harder time getting around. Her limp was becoming more severe. She had sore feet and legs all the time, so we took turns massaging her. I was twelve at the time.

"Grandma?" I rubbed the baby oil on her right leg and started working. "How come your leg hurts so much when you're only sitting down all the time?"

"Oh, I'm just getting old," she laughed.

"But Grandma," I said from my spot on the ground in front of her rocker, "you've been limping for as long as I can remember." I heard her *humph* as I looked up from massaging around her shins to see her frowning and shaking her head. "Oh, sorry. Did that hurt, Grandma?"

"Oh no, no. It's de story."

"What story, Grandma?"

"De story ob why my legs hurt."

♦ ♦ ♦

"Marisa!" my roommate yelled for me at the doorway. "Hurry up! We're going to be late."

"All right. All right. I'm coming. You have the tickets, right?" I asked.

"What? I thought you got them!"

"It was your idea to go, Luisa," I said. "I figured—oh, never mind. Let's go." I grabbed her arm and my bag and headed out the door.

I was dancing alongside the street band with Luisa in tow and a couple of boys, our classmates whom we rode the bus with. I was having a great time, eating and dancing, when I felt a heavy hand on my shoulder and I turned around.

"Carlos!" I greeted my younger brother with a hug and began pulling him toward my friends. "I thought you weren't coming. Come meet these two—"

"How could you be having such a good time when our father could very well be dead?" The music stopped in my head because I realized that could mean only one thing. "Manang, haven't you heard?" Carlos continued solemnly when he saw the shock on my face. "I thought you heard. The Japanese have just bombed Pearl Harbor."

My father was in the U.S. Army and stationed at the Presidio in San Francisco for many years until he was transferred to Schofield Barracks in July of 1941. He left Mother to care for all the children: my three brothers, four sisters, plus three cousins. Oh no, they were not divorced. They loved each other very much, and he wrote to her as often as he could and sent money, too. The benefits were good for our family, and my mother was a good businesswoman, so while we were not rich, we weren't starving. But it was wartime now.

"Nana! Nana! Did you hear?" Carlos and I yelled as we entered our great-aunt's house.

"Anak, I have heard," I heard her reply as she stepped out from the kitchen. "Have you heard from your father?"

"Saan, Nana," I shook my head. "They probably have no time for that now. We'll just have to wait. In the meantime, with the Japanese in control of the Pacific," I explained as I gathered blankets and threw food into them, "their soldiers will be marching in this direction soon. We have to leave now." I saw her already worried face grow long, so I dropped my load and walked over to give her hug.

"Don't worry, Nana. Everything will be fine. Mother is in Pasuquin with the children, so they'll be fine, but we must get you out of here."

The only bag I brought from my uncle's house was Carlos's Boy Scout backpack I had "borrowed" from him years before. The blankets and food were rolled up in there, with some small pictures and little things Nana could grab. She also had a small sack and a light blanket over her shoulders. Carlos was our runner, traveling ahead to see who and what lay before us, and reporting back to us where to go. Aside from his clothes, he had a towel partially tucked into the side of his pants and a black bandanna tied around his head. He relayed for almost two hours before we caught up with another group who had fled from Nana's town. Our big group traveled another day until we heard something.

"Nana, get down!" Carlos pulled both of us to the ground, and Nana rolled into a nearby ditch. I heard the roar of planes overhead. We all pulled our blankets over our heads and I made sure Nana did the same before I completely covered myself. The next thing I heard was bullets from above, hitting the few trees, the dirt, and everything else around us. When the sound of the engines seemed far off, I jumped away from the tree trunk I was leaning against and saw everyone emerge, except Nana. I looked into the ditch and saw a huge lump under her red blanket. When the lump didn't move, I started to panic: the ditch she rolled into was not covered by any trees.

"My God, Nana! Are you all right?" I was pulling at the blanket, scanning it for holes. When I got the blanket loose, I saw that she was still alive, no bullet wounds or anything. Just stunned. "Nana?" I asked, taking her by the shoulders and giving her a mild shake.

"I'm not dead?" she finally asked after a few moments, blinking her eyes and shaking her head in disbelief.

"No, Nana. It's a miracle you're not, especially with that bright blanket you showed those pilots! God's definitely watching us. That's a good sign." I threw the cursed blanket aside and gave her the extra one in my sack.

The rice and fried fish we ate later that evening were barely settled in my stomach when we were on the move again. The American Red Cross set up a shelter at a school. By the time we reached the shelter, more than a day had passed since we left Nana's house. Cots needed to be distributed and set up. Over one hundred people were at the school looking for food and places to sleep. My main concern was for Nana. She was already old and very tired. To keep her nerves from getting rawer with the pushing and shoving, I took charge, making sure everyone in our little group had cots and good places to rest. By the time I was able to lie down to sleep, I couldn't because I was thinking about Father, praying he was okay.

We were asleep for about five hours when a runner bolted in and announced that the Japanese soldiers were crossing the bridge just three miles from the school. We had to evacuate at once. At least everyone else was rested, I thought to myself.

Thirty minutes after we left the shelter, I couldn't keep my eyes open. I had to rest, even for a few minutes. So as the group moved, I lay down next to a sturdy tree trunk. The next thing I knew, I heard shouting and was being shaken awake.

"Manang! Manang, wake up!" Barely able to open my eyes, I was able to make out Carlos's face in front of me and felt his hand on my forehead. "Manang, are you all right? Are you ill? What are you doing?" He shook me by my shoulders again. "Are you okay?"

"I needed some rest. I couldn't stay awake anymore. Just a few minutes more," I pleaded as I lay back down.

"Manang, we must move," Carlos pulled me up. "Here, you can lean on me and when we get to the next shelter or town, I will take care of everything. You sleep tonight." I got up and leaned on my younger brother. We continued on our way.

As we walked, Carlos told me that I had been missing for only fifteen minutes. We caught up to the group quickly because the older members took a longer time to walk. We kept behind a few yards to make sure there were no stragglers. For the next hour or so, I walked using my brother as support. Then I heard a succession of pops from the trees to our right.

"Apo Dios!" The group in front of us yelled, "The Japanese are here! They're firing at us!" People began running in all directions, looking for cover behind trees and bushes. Carlos and I ran ahead looking for Nana. Just as I spotted her hiding behind a pile of logs, my foot got jammed in a tree root. Someone knocked me over from behind, and I felt a sudden intense burning in my right leg, but I kept on running to the small hill where Carlos was. When I slid down next to him he looked at my leg and I saw horror on his face. I followed his stare and nearly fainted. My right shin was the shape of, well, the closest thing is a lopsided L.

Carlos turned my body around so that my head was at the foot of the hill and my legs were pointing to the top to stop the swelling. Later we wondered how I was able to make it to cover up the hill with my leg in such bad shape. I remember lying back against the hill screaming in pain, oblivious to the danger out there. Writhing and cursing, I cried for Mother, something I hadn't done since I was three years old. Carlos, the future brilliant doctor of Pasuquin, gave me a stick to bite on as someone held my head in her lap and I grabbed her hand. Carlos had a firm grip on my ankle and someone else was holding my leg below my knee. Before I could protest, Carlos yanked my leg toward him to straighten the bone and I fainted.

I woke up the next morning on a cot in a nipa hut. I was sweating badly and heard strange voices everywhere. When I opened my eyes, Carlos was sitting next to me on the bed, holding my hand. I asked him what happened.

"Oh, Manang!" He bent down to embrace me. "Thank God, you're all right! When you didn't wake up yesterday, I thought the worst."

"How long have I been out?"

"I'd say about ten hours."

"What?"

"I think your exhaustion, coupled with your broken leg . . ."

"Where are we? Who shot at us? Are Nana and the others all right?" I tried to sit up on my cot, but a splitting headache pulled me back down.

"We're in a guerrilla camp and a member of their group shot at us, thinking we were a troop moving through. No one was hurt but you. Everyone is resting."

"Have you had a chance to—"

"Yes, Manang. I slept right there for a few hours." He nodded his head toward the cot next to me. He couldn't look me in the eye as he spoke, so I asked him what was wrong. "Well, Manang, I tried to set your leg as best as I could. After I straightened it, I tied pieces of dried leaves to your leg with scraps from someone's shirt." I could hear the pain in his voice.

"But?"

"But it's not set correctly. There isn't a doctor in the camp, and we won't be able to get out of here for a few days. By the time we reach a doctor, your bones will be set and they may have to break them again to reset your leg."

I didn't want to think of the pain that was to come when we did reach a doctor, so I changed the subject. "What happened?"

"Their lookout is a fifteen-year-old with specific instructions not to shoot unless shot at. He panicked when he heard the rustling of the leaves and twigs breaking under our feet, and his finger found the trigger before he could think. Right after you blacked out, the leader came out and carried you to their camp."

"Where is the boy now?" I asked, feeling the blackness start to overcome me again.

"He's been crying outside the hut since they brought you in. He feels really bad."

"Tell him not to worry. I'm still alive and so is he . . ." I don't remember anything after that.

◆ ◆ ◆

"But Grandma," I asked with my chin on my hands propped up on the armrests of her chair, "were you ever able to get your leg fixed?" I couldn't look up at her face because my eyes were fixed on the right shin, which had never looked quite right now that I thought about it.

"By the time I got to Pasuquin, de bones fixed demselves togeder, but dey were in de wrong places. De doctor said dat Carlos did a good job, but it could be straighter. Remembering de pain prom before, I told de doctor dat I didn want to do it.

"When I told your daddy and your auntie May, well, dat was de pirst time I saw your daddy cry as a grown man. Dey always ask me about my limp when dey were small, but I didn't like to tell dem because it's painful for me to say, too."

I saw the tears in her eyes when I looked up and hugged her. I always thought her a little crazy, the way she acted. Now I knew.

When I was sixteen, Grandma told me she wanted to go back home. They took Grandpa back in the early eighties when the cancer took over. I realized what this meant, and when I told my parents, they said the arrangements had already been made. This told me that they knew Grandma wasn't going to last much longer. She died nearly three days later on a Thursday. Dad and Auntie May buried her a week and a half later in Pasuquin, Ilocos Norte.

When I was twenty-eight, I had some research to do for my dissertation. I was writing on the effects of colonialism on Philippine literature. I'd never been to the Philippines, but a cousin of mine was getting married, so I thought it would be a good time to meet the rest of the family and get some work done. I went alone. Speaking very little Ilocano (I had opted to take Tagalog in college), I felt very lost. I landed in Manila, knowing from videos and literature that it no longer was the country Grandma told me about. When we drove up through the provinces a week after the wedding, I was expecting to find huge fruit hanging everywhere. I remember asking my cousin who was driving the van where the mango and guava trees were, where the watermelons grew. Everyone in the van gave me weird looks, but no one answered.

When we got to the house, I saw it was a fairly modern two-story wooden house with dirt all around. I shot out of the car looking for the mango tree Grandma said she planted at the rear of the lot as a teenager. The grounds, I saw, were flat, not a tree or vine in sight. I found out that Grandma's younger sister, Lola Glory, had leveled the land fifteen years ago. She had torn out all the plants so that she could make a huge vegetable garden. I walked to the spot where Lola told me the tree used to be, and I squatted next to the vegetables growing there. I gently picked up an eggplant. It was longer than my forearm and as purple as purple could be. Other vegetables I recognized but couldn't name were huge. Grandma held out on me.

Later that afternoon, my family took me to Grandma's and Grandpa's graves. I brought with me some flowers from Lola's garden to place on the headstone. We walked through the cemetery and made our way toward a huge tree in the middle of the field. At the tree, I looked down and saw their names five feet from the trunk:

María Analiza Alonso April 18, 1924–April 8, 1998
Emil V. Alonso April 16, 1919–April 1, 1983
We are the fruit of your love.

I bent over the large headstone above the two graves and placed flowers first on Grandpa's side, wondering about the stories he would have told us if he'd been alive, then on Grandma's. Through my tears, I noticed an oblong object hidden in the grass behind the stone. As I picked it up, I felt the stickiness and recognized the smell that I noticed as I walked to the graves. I was so fixed on finding where Grandma lay that I hadn't noticed what kind of tree was giving her and Grandpa some shade. I walked around the tree, looking for the easiest way up.

As I climbed, I heard my cousins yell, "Hey, what are you doing, Jaime? Don't want to eat those! They grow with the dead people! If you want, we can go to the market to buy them." I didn't pay any attention but reached out from my perch eight feet above the ground. I dropped from eight feet above with a mango the size of my adult hands cupped together. My cousins looked at me like I had lost it.

"Man, she was right!" I laughed. "Jeez, Grandma!" I looked up to the sky as I plopped down next to the headstone with my prize in my hands, my laughter louder. I swore I heard Grandma's laugh as the leaves in the tree above rustled. Me and Grandma.

Note: I would like to thank my cousin, Henry C. Manayan, who coined the title "Land of the Big Fruit" in a speech given at our family reunion.

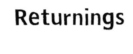

Returnings

Gifts for My Family

Jade Quang Huynh

I'm sending my husband a few packs of special cigarettes.
He will smoke them slowly as if his life were burning away like the
ashes.

I'm sending a few sewing needles to my mother.
She will sew a shirt as if she were sewing through my heart.

I'm sending a few yards of fabric to my sister.
I don't know if she will make a wedding gown or a dress for a
funeral.

I'm sending my brother a lot of candy.
He will eat so many sweets because his life is so bitter.

I'm sending my father a plain white shirt.
He will wear it only once when he goes to his execution.

I'm sending to Vietnam an ocean of tears.
I'm sending to Vietnam a dream of a peaceful day.

I'm sending my husband a fountain pen.
He will paint his life as a dream drawn between the thin lines.

I'm sending my mother a few boxes of tea.
She will pour me some tea as her eyes run out of tears.

I'm sending my sister a few matches.
She will burn her life in an empty, cold, and misty place.

I'm sending my brother a lovely ring.
He will sell it to find a way to escape his life.

I'm sending my father a few bottles of sleeping pills.
He will use them to lull himself to sleep in the jail cell where he
is imprisoned for life.

I'm sending to Vietnam a caring song.
I'm sending to Vietnam my dreams of a peaceful sleep.

Translated by Jade Quang Huynh

Ang Tunay na Lalaki
Receives a Package from Home

Nick Carbo

and out of the layers of newspapers pops up
the wooden statue of La Virgen del Pelo Mojado.
The note attached to her feet is from his mother
reminding him, "*Querido hijo,* the reason
why you may have not yet found a wife
is that you don't go to church. This is a replica
of our town's miraculous Virgin. She will help you.
Pray to her, *hijo.* The wife will come."
Ang Tunay na Lalaki is sure his mother has arranged
for a novena for the next six months at their church.
He can't bear to think of the whole town including
him in their prayers—"Please Holy Mother, help
Lalakito find a good American wife."

The next day, he notices all sorts of women smiling
at him on the streets of New York. An auburn-haired
woman with a French accent asks him directions
to the Armani Exchange store. An Indian woman
in a sari asks him for the time. Even a group
of perfume-scented Filipinas stops him on Mercer
looking for the swanky Cendrillon restaurant.

On the N train, he hands a couple of quarters
to a homeless woman, who says, "Que Dios
te bendiga. Tu mujer te está esperando."
Your woman is waiting for you. The train swerves,
he grabs a pole to steady himself. He looks
for the homeless woman, but she's gone.
He wants to know where she's waiting for him.

Back at his apartment he finds no fancy-looking letters
in his mailbox, no messages on his answering machine.
He takes La Virgen del Pelo Mojado from the floor,
places her on the mantelpiece, and begins
to arrange the flowers he bought in two tall
water glasses which he will place on both sides
of his miraculous Virgin of the Wet Hair.

The Terno

Aurora Harris

In Detroit, at the top of the stairs,
in the small room with books,
clothes strewn on the floor,
I put on Mother's terno.[1]
Not the one that smells of mothballs.
The one that smells like fresh
gutted relatives
bombs
burned sampaguita.[2]

This terno is special.
There are voices hemmed in it.
Tears stitched into batik
double knotted on the seams—
the growled accusations of being a spy,
a chorus of morning prayers swept away by
imperial tongues—
Ohayoo gozaimasu[3]
ano ba ang gustomo
Capitan san?[4]

When I smooth the wrinkles,
the terno clings and moans.
When I tinikling[5] through the darkness
of Mother's buried secrets,
her open wounds don't sleep
and she asks me to stop
the nightmares.

She never told me
that our history, the dead
would hold me hostage
in screaming holes
with livers exposed by bayonets.

I'll remember
for you, Ma, and
no one will come
and get you. I
still have my boning
knife. I'll kill
collaborators before
they reach
the porch.

Notes

[1] Terno: the woman's native dress of the Philippines.
[2] Sampaguita: the national flower of the Philippines.
[3] Japanese: Good morning.
[4] Tagalog and Japanese: What would you like, Captain sir?
[5] Tinikling: a Filipino dance performed with bamboo or cane sticks.

Granddaughter

Fiona Cheong

Outside my brother's window, areca palms breathing light and wind push easily through the air, trunks the bleached gray of driftwood growing in the neighbor's yard across the street. All his neighbors' houses are low, I notice, sprawling like those houses the British used to build *back there* when we were colonized (or rather, when our parents and grandparents were, our great-grandparents, great-great-grandparents—my brother and I know which houses because they were still around in our childhood, though occupied by Chinese families by then). His neighbors' houses are simpler, however, with walls pale-painted in placid, unfettered shades of white or yellow, and no verandas. A few have small, screened-in front porches. Among such houses, my brother's house stands out a little, red-brick and narrow as an urban townhouse, the only two-story house on the block. It looks a little transplanted, I think. Like him, like us when I'm here, though I don't tell him this when he asks, "So, what do you think?" I say, "So, this is Florida," like someone reading from a movie script.

He knows I haven't answered his question: what do I think of his house, of his living room, his furniture, the way he's got things set up? He's searching my face in that old way, waiting to hear what I see as though he can't be sure, otherwise, can't trust his own choices, can't believe what he sees when he sees it alone. His uncertainty knocks on the inside of my heart, something I know I understand but I cannot recall what, precisely, I understand about it. I'm remembering being teenagers with him, how I would lay out his clothes, match colors for him before a date, as though he were color-blind, as though he hadn't already proved to all of us that he was the artist, like our mother. My brother no longer admits this about himself, what he was, what he might still be. His college degree is in aerospace and aeronautical engineering, from the University of Notre Dame. He holds a master's in mechanical engineering from FIT— "That's the Florida Institute of Technology," he tells me. He points out that he's now enrolled part-time in FIT's M.B.A. program, and the company he works for is financing his education. I know only that it's some kind of engineering design corporation, with offices in cities that sound to him like home—Taiwan, Hong Kong, Manila, and especially Kuala Lumpur, from which it is less than an hour's flight to Singapore, on commuter planes that take off every hour. My brother works in sales. He is good at this, has always been good with strangers, always sold the most raffle tickets, collected the most money on Flag Day, raised the longest list of sponsors for the national 5K race. He also saw colors I couldn't see, was able in kindergarten to pick out "mauve" without hesitation, identify its crayon shade like the face of a longtime cousin. He drew in the corners of our relatives' living room walls if nobody was watching—inch-long, perfectly proportioned combat soldiers parachuting down to the parquet flooring, emergency Red Cross helicopters circling above, the darker spin of propellers dipping into the white or yellow painted brick. ("No matter how I check him before we go out, he always manages to smuggle along a pencil," my mother would say, apologizing. Eventually, our relatives began storing drawing paper in their homes.) I remember this fact about my brother, a puzzle I have not been able to finish. It sinks like an anchor in the room, its iron weight holding us in between.

"This is a good time to be here," he says, looking out the window and nodding at the arecas, wondering in the back of his mind what to do with me for the rest of the day. I realize he hasn't planned ahead. He never did. I check my watch. It's barely half past two, only midafternoon. "Especially for you guys," he goes on. "Get away from the winter. See how warm it is? I told you, right?" He turns and glances for the sixth or seventh time around the living room, which is separated from the kitchen by a tiled staircase with a wooden banister on one side. On the side without a banister, my brother has turned the lower steps into shelves, stacking telephone directories and restaurant coupons on the edges.

"It's so sunny here," I say, wanting to help out. "David's going to love it." I remind myself that David will arrive on Wednesday, only four days away. I check my watch again. I'm wearing the Mickey Mouse, my play watch, a Valentine's Day gift from David two years back, the one I strap on when the last week of classes begins, to remind myself the semester is ending, that it's almost Christmas, or almost summer. Because I don't play well and never have, was told even by the sisters at St. Agnes (my mother's alma mater and mine) that I was too serious for a child. David thought the Mickey Mouse would help, American Mickey with his banana-colored shoes and his red shorts bright as strawberries in June, his silly pose, his silly smile. I finger the length of his body behind the glass. It was David who insisted that Joshua and I needed some time alone, not having seen each other in almost five years.

"You know what? I think I need a nap, man," my brother says.

I take the cue. "You haven't been sleeping well?" I ask, looking up.

Joshua shakes his head, his hair falling slightly over his left eye. He wears it longer than he would be allowed to in Singapore, longer than I have ever seen it. We have different hair, I notice. His is loose and soft, and he wears it in one even length. Like Bruce Lee, I imagine him thinking. His hair covers his ears, almost brushes his shoulders. My hair won't fit that cut. On girls and women it's worn with bangs and called the *china-doll,* but my hair's an anomaly among Chinese hair, too stiff, too thick. (It was Suzy, my mother's hair-dresser, who pointed this out. "Must be my fault," my mother sighed. "Must be I rubbed too much olive oil into her scalp when she was a baby. But I was so afraid she was going to have thin hair like me. I didn't want her to become *botak,* you know." *Botak,* the Malay word for bald. At eleven, I was still bilingual, still understood her back-and-forth linguistic switches.) Joshua's hair is also darker than mine. It is black, looks like real Asian hair, looks authentic. According to my passport, mine is black, black, too, according to my driver's license, but this must be because on both occasions, the clerk simply assumed, didn't think to look, couldn't be bothered, or couldn't find a reason to care. I know it's an inaccurate description because some gray has started to appear, three or four strands that I've noticed, and when I asked Sherry, my hairdresser in Pittsburgh, if coloring my hair would ruin it in any way, dry it out like a perm, she told me I needn't start coloring it yet, that the gray isn't noticeable, but later I should use Clairol Loving Care, darkest brown. Sherry tells me not to choose black, that my hair isn't black.

"Took my last exam yesterday," Joshua says.

I nod. "How'd it go?"

"Good." He nods, the hair still grazing his left eye. He doesn't push it away. "I think I'm going to get all A's." He laughs, checking my face to see if I'm surprised. I don't know if I am, but I try not to be. I smile back. I'm not sure what he sees, but I keep smiling, and he goes on. "Can you imagine? Me? Getting all A's? Wait till Mum and Dad hear about this. But maybe don't tell them till the results come out for sure." His voice has turned somber, as if he's forgotten we're not there anymore, not still in that house, not children. The moment lasts a second, two seconds. Then he remembers. He smiles out the window. I watch him brush the hair off his forehead. When he turns to me again, there's no mistaking the relief in his eyes. "So, do you mind if I take a nap?" he asks.

"I'm going to take one, too," I say, standing up.

"Really? Oh, okay." He remains seated, processing this new information. I know what's going through his head. His sister doesn't take naps, never took naps. Is something wrong with her? Is she sick? ("I always know when Anna's sick," our mother said, when I was fifteen and caught some strange strain of the flu, lost twelve pounds, and had headache attacks for six months. "That day I came home and found her lying down, I knew at once she was sick. Anna never goes to lie down in the afternoon. Too much impatience in her.")

"Late night," I say, because Joshua hears her, too. I know he does. I keep talking. "I had to finish grading papers. Didn't want to bring them with me, you know."

He nods, not sure whether to believe what I have said, even though he knows it makes perfect sense. His own semester has just ended, and his professors are at their desks, armed with pens and endless cups of coffee. But something old taps on the inside of my brother's heart as well, fear consistent as a loud-ticking clock. "You've lost weight, you know," he says, his tone abrupt, accusing. "You're not on a diet or something, are you?"

"I'm quite fit," I say. "Don't worry." As if to prove the point, I sling my pocketbook over my head and across my chest, then turn to where we have left my bags slumped against the wall. I lift my laptop onto my left shoulder, then heave the garment bag onto my right, even though they are not equally weighted and don't quite balance me. All that's left is my knapsack, which has my books. I look at Joshua and am about to ask if he will get that, the sentence already full-formed before my eyes, a line I am borrowing from normal circumstances, when a movement outside the window catches my attention. But when I turn my head, it is gone.

"What?" Joshua asks. He comes over, leans down, picks up my knapsack, and dangles it by his side, carrying my books like air.

"I thought I saw something," I say, and wonder what exactly makes him ask, what my face shows.

"Like what?" he says.

Outside the window, sun steams over the grass, the light damp with humidity, thick as monsoon water building. No one has appeared on the street—I am not sure why this seems significant, but it does—or at the neighbor's windows on the other side. Nothing moves, except the same slight wind in the neighbor's yard, the arecas flicking the soft tips of their leaves like women's sighs. Time caresses the air, subtle and dangerous as longing, and I turn back to my brother. "It's nothing," I say, shaking my head. "Just my imagination."

But Joshua isn't looking at me. He's staring, instead, at my garment bag, wondering if he could demand I let him carry it.

I turn and start up the stairs—his stairs, I realize, but I do not stop, even though I have no idea which room I am to sleep in. A second later, I hear him behind me, following.

♦ ♦ ♦

We do not know what happened. We do not have the facts. Perhaps she first laid eyes on him in a bar, Maxim's, or Le Rendez-vous, or the Copacabana—those were some of their names, I've been told. It was 1942, World War II, the year before the Japanese took over. Singapore was swarming with soldiers, blue- and brown-eyed British and Australian men, all hanging out in bars because ours was their rest–and-recreation country. It would have been the likely site of the meeting, a bar, though not even my father knows for sure (he was four and a half when she left—this is all he remembers, he says, or all he will tell us). I carry a vague sense of location, compelling and shadowed as first memory, of smoke-layered, murmuring rooms falling off the sides of hotel lobbies, a back door that opened to a cement garden path—downtown, where all the bars were. A hibiscus bush, the blush-red petals having begun their wilt at the end of the day, now wrinkling shut, slow resignation in moonlight. Periwinkle slipping off the edges of the path, their whiteness dusty against the dark. Perhaps she needed to step out for air. Or, he had

179

suggested it. "Let's get some air." But no, that would have been too rough. "Would you like to get some air?" Possibly. "Shall we step out for some air?" His Australian accent riding the smoke and chatter, full of another country, the shining possibilities for escape. She had nodded, yes, but not too eagerly. She already knew she wanted more than a one-night stand. Enough of those. He had taken her hand, led her through the crowd, pulled her gently around a stumbling drunk, a uniformed corporal only slightly younger than himself—there were so many of them, so many that looked like him. He knew this, knew he had to do something different, separate himself somehow from them, for her. He chose to be gentle. A gamble. She had already told him, her husband was very gentle. It was what she loved about him.

◆ ◆ ◆

When the audio signal from my laptop hits the air, it's a piano key, a softly vibrating pulse, comfortable in its consistency, its sameness of pitch and tone. When the screen is set, I drive the short, darting arrow straight to Kermit Unix, and double-click, my thumb and finger moving so easily, I think I could manage this now without looking. I dial in when the terminal window opens, type my user-name and password, and remind myself it's a long-distance call.

Light washes across the screen, and the sun explodes, quiet as wind over water. My e-mail inbox contains three new messages, the most recent from my department chair. I scan the other two names again and then stand to pull the shade. The sky's a prairie, flatter and wider than it ever is in Pittsburgh. The arecas have settled to a blinding green stillness, their fronds stiff in the air. I allow myself a moment to survey the street, my brother's street, where he's been living these five years. More pastel houses, innocuous as toys, and neat, sunny, square lawns postcard-perfect along the block. No fences. More trees, more spindle-leafed palms, and squat palms with shocks of leaves, and taller palms with slim gray trunks arching up into willow heads. The sweetness of recognition wells up inside me, so I tell myself at first that I recognize the trees. But I don't know their names and realize it is only their likeness I recognize. They are not the same trees.

I tell myself to read David's message first, and when I return to the desk, it is what I intend. But my finger slips, or perhaps my heart has somehow lost its vigilance. I am careless. The arrow lands on her name. I am acutely aware of risk, but I cannot drag it away, danger beckoning like something shiny-wet the tide is just now bringing in. I look down a second, see my thumb like someone else's thumb. I hear more than feel the double-click.

♦ ♦ ♦

That night, there was no possibility she would stay. Too many vacuous afternoons, hours of watching the sun slide shadows across the polished ramin boards of the veranda floor, lean shapes of tree limbs falling inches from her toes, each day's light passing east from the sago palm west to the jacaranda—the blossoming jacaranda, where dusk after dusk the same birds had gathered, their tiny dark bodies huddling, hovering, oppressive as family eyes, peering among the leaves. Too much, her sipping cup after solitary cup of oolong tea shipped specially from China, that token of wedding vows entering slowly and almost painless, blunt as a letter opener beneath her wife sheath. When it had come apart, that sheath shredding like a cheap dress, still new but unwearable, she had hardly noticed, had found herself one afternoon, about to step onto the veranda and thinking (the thought sudden as a stray bullet), no. Just that. No.

I imagine she intended to break the news face-to-face: Hock Siew, I'm leaving. The words floating aimlessly above the undisturbed bed had probably been chosen so carefully (the simpler, the more straightforward, the better), practiced nights before that night. But she had miscalculated, perhaps mistaken time's density for lateness in the garden's shadows outside the bar, had come home too early on the arm of her Australian lieutenant (he waiting in the backseat of the taxi, his eyes closed for a minute, his doll-blond head resting on the beige imitation leather). Perhaps it was too much Johnny Walker in her veins dulling her senses, though it wouldn't be believed likely that she was drunk. Too classy for that— she, too, must have heard this, a thousand and one times. What a classy wife Tay Hock Siew had found himself. Envy from both the men and the women.

In any case, he wasn't there ("Your grandfather never left his poker game before two in the morning"). It must have crossed her mind to leave a note, some kind of explanation, some kind of good-bye. For Hock Siew, still her husband, whom she did still love (packing their small, gold-framed wedding photo between her lingerie so that the glass wouldn't get scratched). For Pancake, Boy-boy, and Eliza, all fast asleep now, she thought. Her children. Her babies. But there wasn't time for a note, not with a taxi meter running. (What if Patrick started wondering if she was taking advantage of him, using him for his money? So many of the local women were doing that, giving those playboy soldiers tit for tat.) It had taken her much patience and hard work to come upon one like Patrick, the marrying kind. Already, she could discern this in him, a distant calmness in his gaze, that long, deep sense of a future, the care with which he measured what he said, as if it mattered to him that he didn't lie or leave a false impression.

A real letter would be better, she told herself. Two letters, one to Hock Siew and one to Pancake, because Pancake was the eldest and would have to explain it to the other two—she knew her husband couldn't be depended on to do it. He might explain, or he might not, might say simply, "Your mum's not coming home anymore, that's all I know." Tomorrow, she told herself, she would take care of everything. There would be time. Two letters, one to Hock Siew, one to Pancake.

She lifted her bag off the bed, turned off the light, stepped out into the corridor and turned toward the children's rooms, paused, changed her mind, and quietly, her heart fluttering, turned the other way.

◆ ◆ ◆

Joshua wonders why it's taken me so long. I know he does. Perhaps he even wonders, why now, finally? But being my brother, and the younger, he won't ask. Such information he's used to not having, is accustomed to sticking into the blanks variations of the usual, easy explanation—too busy, too much work, maybe next summer, maybe Christmas. ("You know Anna, always putting her studies first," my mother would tell relatives in the beginning, saving face before their unflinching gaze. "And it's good. You see? I don't have to worry about her." The excuse cannot be easy to maintain, can be countered—"Allah-mak, Gracie, your daughter graduated how many years ago? See-lah how successful she is, already one book published, right? Tell her she can afford to take a holiday. It's high time she comes home." But I know my mother, a proud woman. Her face doesn't collapse in public. "Anna's a university professor, can you imagine? Can you imagine that daughter of mine, teaching English to American students?")

I wonder what Joshua would say if I were to tell him everything. I wonder what I would tell him. I wonder what everything might be.

◆ ◆ ◆

There ended up being no letters—there wouldn't be for years, but she couldn't have known this, couldn't have anticipated what was to come. She must have tried to write. Alone for the afternoon, the slim gold-plated Shaeffer poised above the blank sheet on the narrow hotel desk, she must have tried. Waiting for just the right words, staring out the window at the weathered building across the alley. I imagine she would have chosen such a room, positioned discreetly in the back, preferably a corner room with only one shared wall. Nothing facing the front road, local traffic, the accidental gaze of a relative who might happen to pass on the sidewalk, look up at the wrong moment—an unlikely event, but a woman with so much at stake could not have taken the risk. It would have been the afternoon, or no later than late morning. Half-past eleven, perhaps, or a few minutes to noon. He would not have left before then, having stayed the night, though there was the matter of his showing up on time for work, the necessity of his continuing to fulfill his duties as a naval officer (she would have made sure of this, would not have jeopardized her ticket out). They had probably made love before he got up to shave (she leaning in the bathroom doorway then, slightly fascinated—her husband, having a generally hairless Chinese face, never shaved), and then he had gone out, her Australian Patrick, and brought back breakfast from the market two blocks away, a packet of steaming chee-cheong-fun noodles with the sweet red sauce she loved, sesame seeds generously sprinkled on because he had been willing to pay the hawker twenty cents extra for that. And coffee, strongly brewed, with condensed milk. Ask for kopi-susu, she had said. No more oolong tea. Crossing oolong tea out of her life forever, the decision falling like a steel gate in her heart.

The Japanese had already invaded Thailand, were already mapping out the Thai-Malay border. He must have known, had heard the rumors, had requested transfer papers for himself. Probably, he had considered the potential complications the night before, but only briefly. Before he had maneuvered his way toward the bar, stepped deliberately through the swaying crowd keeping her at a safe distance across the room, the perfumed necks and sweaty faces, shimmering lipstick, a touch of mascara leaking here and there, the vagrant hand on his arm—he must have suspected nothing would be simple. Her papers, their courtship, everything having to be rushed under the circumstances. But all this, only if he were to fall in love. That, perhaps, had been his error. He had not expected to fall in love, nor anticipated a woman who would rearrange his dreams in the middle of the night, weave them so tightly, so effortlessly, with her own, owning them already, their first night. Then, a second error. He must have believed he knew our culture, how women like us don't leave our families. Telling himself, he'd had enough affairs to know.

No one was ever prepared to come upon my grandmother. She caught us all off guard.

The Maid

Eugene Gloria

From America my sister writes about the latest action on the wing—
    she lists: lazuli bunting, yellow-breasted chat,
        magpie, tufted titmouse, and vesper sparrow.

Binoculars in one hand, she whiles away hours on winding trails,
    still as a sentinel, serious as a reprimand.
        But here in Manila, where fresh air is as rare as tonic water

and the heat as steady as Kurosawa's rain,
    I've given in to air-conditioned cinemas and crowded malls,
        shoulder to shoulder with the progeny of American TV.

Once a girl in rubber slippers walked into a restaurant
    to order some takeout for her small charge.
        The girl, no more than a child, spied

the room full of oval tables and bright people clad
    in brighter church dresses and Sunday shoes.
        Gaudy matrons with cellular phones

while I, in my polo shirt and penny loafers,
    watched her as my sister would
        trail the still flight of a hummingbird.

If a messenger of the Lord were to intercede and tell this girl
    to walk away and never look back,
        would she vanish into a grain of salt among the nameless?

But when her gaze locked into mine, her eyes widened
    like the mouth of an animal about to swallow its prey—
        it was saying, *I know you, I know you.*

Becoming American

Expurgation

Elizabeth Gordon

Sometimes, Mommy got sad
and she'd cut herself
out of the family
photos she had tenderly
arranged (six or eight
per page) using those
black paper triangles, each
licked and fitted and
pressed to the thick
heavy sheets of our
thick heavy family album.
Leaning on the arm
of our orange vinyl
sofa, the book splaying
across her short thighs,
she would remove, carefully,
the photographs she meant
to maim, using her
long polished fingernails to
pry them from permanence,
and with scissors shining
in her left hand,
upside down, she would
cut her face out
from the rest of
our faces, out of
some moment in time.
It could be Easter
morning, all of us
posing in stiff clothes
by the flowering dogwood
before going to Mass;
it could be someone's
six-year-old birthday,

someone puffy-cheeked, blowing
out yellow spiral candles
on a ballerina cake.
It didn't matter; Mommy
would cut, cut, cut
deep in a taut
and furious trance, her
hands swift but steady,
her mouth and jaw
set so tight it
looked like she had
bitten her own flesh
and couldn't let go.
She'd keep on cutting
until the tremble took
her lips and at
last the tears slipped
through, and once the
spell had broken, she
would fling the album
onto the floor and
stand, scissors still dangling
from forefinger and thumb,
and stare without belief
at what she couldn't
undo, but had done.
Later, ugly, sobbing, she
would tuck the wounded
photos into their black
slings, then gather the
glossy scraps of herself
(some the size of
half dollars, others no
bigger than baby teeth)
and toss every piece,
each smiling face, where
the trash would go.
And when it was

happening, and when it
was through, I never
knew, and I couldn't
imagine why, Mommy would
try to rip out
the evidence of herself
in our family's life,
the golden new life
she felt so lucky
to be living in
this great God-blessed
country, where she was
free to be anything,
anything at all, except—
now I see—what
she already had been.

Waiting for Orders

Geronimo G. Tagatac

We were shadows, moving softly through the North Carolina pine forests, stopping, checking our maps against our compasses, listening, whispering to each other. Then setting off again, feeling our way forward. In my mind, I would raise the ground to eye level and tell myself that here was where the southwest hills would tip me to the southeast, where the map showed I would intersect a curve in a rail line, or come to a place overlooking a highway.

Some nights, the rain would come and we knew that while it lasted we were safe to sleep soundly under our ponchos. The dry nights, though, were filled with expectation mixed with the smell of pine. The "aggressor forces" liked to move then. Those nights we would wait for the burst of lingering light that meant one of their patrols had tripped the wire on a flare. There would be footfalls, shouts, and quick muzzle flashes from the blanks in our weapons, explosions from grenade simulators, and the smell of burned powder in the air. And then we would move again, through the folds and veils of the forest, to the edge of a clearing, staying just inside the shadows of the treeline, listening to the distant sound of a car or watching some civilian walk boldly down a sunlit road, until darkness came and it was time to practice blowing another bridge, derailing a train, ambushing one more convoy. We were twenty days in the field that July.

On the twenty-first day, a radio message came, "Rendezvous with trucks, tomorrow, 0900 hours." It was followed by a set of grid coordinates. We ate the last of the hoarded graham crackers, the final, precious halves of candy bars, and moved across the forest in the new yellow light of the last day. The trucks came and took us back to Fort Bragg, where the streets are laid out in square patterns, back to hot water, white sheets, and the crunch of evenly raked gravel beneath our boots on the company street. It was good to shower and put on a clean, starched fatigue blouse with my last name, "Guerrero," above the left pocket. We took our field fatigues, smelling of wood smoke and dried sweat, to the post cleaners. For a while, we could walk in the light and cross open spaces again. We could talk in normal voices and laugh out loud.

What we talked about increasingly were missions, combat assignments to the only war going: Vietnam. A lack of a mission was something that separated us from the older men, who wore the combat infantryman's badge with its silver rifle and wreath on a blue background, on their dress uniforms. To us, the promise of war was the finale, the shape behind the shadow, the reason for the months in the field. Combat enveloped in a strange silence those, like First Sergeant Miller, who had fought in Europe, Korea, and Vietnam. The experience gave their faces the quiet look of eternal repose that one sees on ancient statues. A mission was something that came at reveille, after roll call and announcements, when First Sergeant Miller, in a rumbly voice, would read a list of names from his clipboard and say, "You got orders today."

We took four days of leave. Lopez wanted Greensboro because it had a women's college. I was thinking about Myrtle Beach, with its warm water and dance clubs. James talked about his mother's house, in the suburbs of Baton Rouge. Free place to stay, he said. He talked about shooting pool at Sammy's and the great free sausages they served. He raved about the LSU coeds and talked about going up to Jackson, Mississippi, to watch his cousin, Dieter, race his car on the Jackson flat track. So, we took the standby flight to New Orleans. As the airliner made its final approach into the airport outside of New Oreans, I watched green bayous flash beneath us and wondered if that was what Vietnam would be like.

After a day and a night in Baton Rouge, we grew restless. So we drove up to Jackson for the flat track races. Dieter was a tall skinny guy in his early twenties, just growing his first mustache. I could tell he was in awe of us, but he didn't let it show. He didn't try to make a big deal out of being a race car driver either. I took a quick liking to him. After the race, we watched Dieter's crew load his car onto a trailer and disappear into the night. Then Lopez, James, and I took Dieter to a bar and knocked back a few beers. We'd gotten hungry by about one in the morning and had gone into a café for grits and eggs, where we flirted with the waitress and got thrown out by the guy who ran the place. It turned out the waitress was his wife. Who gave a shit? They were nothing but a couple of locals wrapped up for life in their ten-table dive. We'd have missions halfway around the world in a month or two. What the hell did a jealous husband in

Jackson rate compared to night drops over North Carolina, mock ambushes in the forest, and a war halfway around the world?

It was three in the morning when we started south from Jackson. Dieter was behind the wheel of the big white sedan, driving with one lazy arm over the top of the steering wheel, moving us down the road fast, the car lifting up over the little rises in the highway, settling back down, taking the slack out of the suspension system. Very easy, very cool. And we'd settled down, James in the front seat next to Dieter, me in the back with Lopez, because it was hours back to Baton Rouge, and there was nothing to do but fall back into your seat and let the road and the heat take you off into the depths of the night. All the windows were rolled down and the dark air was blowing in, onto our sure faces and tanned arms. Across the fields, you could see the thickest part of night tangled up in the groves of trees, waiting for the hours to pass and for daylight to set it free.

Dieter took the sedan through a long, fast turn, and up over a gentle rise. I felt myself lighten as we crested the rise, and our headlights shot off high above the road's surface, reaching out into the darkness above the Mississippi earth. And then the beams dropped onto a man lying on his back, less than twenty feet in front of us, his left knee raised as though he were just thinking about getting up.

Dieter never had a chance to touch the brakes. We went over him. The sound, just inches below us, was that of something running over a pile of thin, dried branches. And then there was nothing but the sound of big car tires singing on the asphalt, the wind, and Lopez's soft accented voice saying, "Jesus Christ! That was a man!"

"Stop," I said. "We've got to go back. Stop."

Dieter pulled the car over and stopped. Then I was out of the car, running hard to cover the hundred yards between us and what I knew was lying out there, cooling on the warm asphalt. I don't know why I was running because I must have known that he was dead. Nobody could have survived that. And then it came to me, that I'd never seen a man killed.

I could smell the blood and torn flesh before I reached him. I looked down at the shape lying in the road. He looked as though something had shaken him out, dropped him onto the road's surface, and then kicked him hard, twenty-five feet along the asphalt. There wasn't a pulse or a breath of life in him.

I waited until Lopez reached me, shook my head to his unspoken questions, and sent him back to the silent car, where James sat with Dieter, both of them stunned. I told Lopez to get Dieter to drive him and James down the highway to the next town and to phone the police. Then I walked over to embankment on the side of the road, sat down, and waited for the police to arrive.

I sat in the thick, humid air waiting for the dawn, frightened of what the sun would show me, but wanting the sun to rise so that I'd know east from west. I could smell the spirit of the dead man hovering about his body and my body, and feel him soaking into the fabric of my shirt and the threads of my Levi's, trying to hold onto the texture of life for as long as he could. I wanted the rain to come and wash the smell of him out of my clothes and shoes. I wanted the light to come, to claim his spirit and to show me his torn face.

I sat there trying to figure out what the hell he'd been waiting for. Maybe he'd had too much to drink and passed out in the middle of the road, or decided to kill himself over some sweet, uninterested girl in town or on the next farm. I looked beyond him, into the fields where the first light was giving shape to a distant treeline. I told myself that I'd probably see lots of bodies once I got a mission, Vietnamese bodies, dead Americans. I would have to get used to the sight of killed men because it was part of what I would be doing. I imagined what it would be like to sit beside James's dead body, or Lopez's corpse. I wondered what it would be like to try to hold on to the sound of James's voice, his laughter, his jokes, and the look in his eyes when we talked.

A car came up the road. I stood up, walked out to the middle of the lane, in front of the dead man, to wave the car around him, to protect him from any further harm. The car slowed and came alongside me, and I saw the face of a middle-aged woman peer through the open, front passenger window. The smell and sight of the body hit her and I saw her mouth open, elongating her face in horror. Her pale hands came up quickly, covered her face, and the car accelerated away.

There was enough light to see his smashed face. I couldn't tell much about him. He was a white man with dark hair, about as tall as me, and slim. I wondered if I might be looking down on a prophetic image of myself dying in war, lying outside some hamlet with an unpronounceable name, bloody shirt torn open, legs broken at odd angles, head thrown back, arms flung out as if frozen in some final dive through space. What if war's nothing but chance? I thought.

The edge of the sun was burning the last of the night away when James, Lopez, and Dieter got back, followed by a police car and an ambulance. It took an hour for the police to finish questioning us, to take photographs of the body in the road, to write their preliminary reports. Afterward, the ambulance crew lifted the body gently into a black rubber body bag, zipped it up, put the bag in the ambulance, and drove away. None of us had ever seen a body bag before.

We drove south toward Baton Rouge all through the hot morning in silence. Dieter hit the brakes hard once when a small animal raced across the road in front of us. When we got back to James's mother's place, we had coffee, packed our bags, and tried to sleep. Dieter took us to the airport the next morning, dropping us off in front of the terminal. He said little except, "Bye. You take care, now." We flew back to North Carolina and caught the bus to Fort Bragg. We were silent during the whole journey back.

A few days later, we read about the accident in the Fayetteville paper. The dead man was twenty-one. Younger than any of us. He'd been married and divorced, no children, lived alone. His name was withheld pending notification of his family. There was no explanation of why he'd been lying in the middle of a dark road between Jackson and Baton Rouge, at three in the morning.

A month later, as we stood for reveille in the cool, early air, on the clean gravel of the company street, the first sergeant called us to attention. He told us in a voice that was almost gentle, "Guerrero, James, Lopez. You got orders."

Sacrifice Is the Key to Heaven

M. G. Sorongon

Lent comes early in 1980. February, which doesn't matter
since February, March, and even April are one season in Michigan.
After Mass, we troop back into our classroom, sit at our seats,
stare at the ashes on the forehead of the girl sitting across.
Galoshes make a squeaky, pleasant rubbing against linoleum.
We redo the bulletin board: take down the doilies, the pink cut-out hearts,
each creased down the middle just so, like an insect.
Miss Shea hands out green construction paper (she should be saving it
for St. Patrick's, but there's plenty, and Miss Shea is as generous
as she is wide) and we trace from a stencil the shape of a key.

Lissa Wendler's giving up meat, because she doesn't like it anyway.
John Carrico swears off Ding Dongs. The Basil twins say good-bye to Atari
and ice cream (or is it ice cream and Atari?). Rich, pious
Laura Egleston, always different, says she's doing something
extra instead of giving up—she's practicing the piano every
day. James Purcell says that's dumb, but then, when pressed, won't tell his.
David Schnurstein,
the only Jew in our class (in the school?), says he
doesn't have to give up anything, anything at all, and sits
with his arms folded, smug and left out again. Andy Moon says he's
giving up his allowance. Allowance! we cry, anguished. Aaron

Knieper (who goes on to play in the minor leagues) says he's giving up
his dog and baseball. No fair: you've already given up baseball. We point to
the icy streets outside. And anyway, how can you give up
a dog? It would die. I look out the window and decide to give
up pizza-flavored Combos—cheese-filled pretzels that give you swift entrance
into the cafeteria in-crowd. (Is there an "in-crowd" in second
grade?) One of the Basil twins asks if you can be that
specific: don't you have to give up all Combos, even the Cheddar,
the Nacho? If she can do that, can I just give up Frogger,
but not Space Invaders? Miss Shea tells us to hush and passes out

scissors. I get lefty ones, and struggle to tear paper: is it better
to cut with the right hand, or to try the uncomfortable, sinister left?
My key ends up with a rip in one of the teeth. We labor
over our green keys, print our sacrifices with Magic Marker.
(Laura E. does cursive and i's dotted with hearts.) Then, one by one, we
trot up, staple our best loves to the yellow cork. There, amid old stubborn
staples our keys form a spiral: each blessed, holy
offering moving out, and out, ashes and dust, and we stand back, dazed
and wondering if, after the forty days, we're supposed to rejoice
at reunion with those loves, or realize, Alleluia, no,

we didn't really need them at all, or in the first place. We stand back,
unsure, and lightly touch the fading smudges on our foreheads,
just to make sure they're still there.

New Territory: A Sestina

M. G. Sorongon

U.S. Highways 82, 43, 11: they weave a wandering web
across the laminated Alabama map. You'd think the trivial dust
of rural roads would choke me, that the full, clean sweep
of the big city routes would eclipse this happy vacuum.
But no: the berry-like clusters of houses off I-20 hold no spell
on me. It's the country I adore—a wide opening door

set back from a small two-lane county road, a door
that, when entered, reveals the plain and simple web
of small rooms and glowing television. "Sit a spell,"
the hausfrau invites. I take the company chair. "Do you dust
often?" I ask, and grip the handle of my imperious vacuum,
that noble beast at my side. I allow my eyes to sweep

the dim, coarse room. The minutes creep. To sweep
away the silence, she coughs, looks out the metal screen door
at the pregnant dog in the yard. My hostess's eyes are a vacuum
as she hands me a tumbler of sweet tea. I wipe the web
of sweat from my brow and balance my dust-
ridden hat on a knee. I stand, and begin to spell

out my spiel. And here is where the spell,
the real magic, begins: I dance like a chimney sweep,
fling coffee grounds, eggshells, pennies, spices' dust
from the grimy kitchen to the broken screen door.
A crowning touch: the dregs of my iced tea, making a web
of dark wet across the dingy carpet. Then, the vacuum

is plugged in, and the house shakes as if in the vacuum
of a hurricane. The roar of the great beast casts its own spell,
worries, doglike, from the room and the lady's mind, webs
in far corners. I click the switch, offer a moment of silence, sweep
a showcasing hand along the carpet's pile. And even when the door
is held open for me, the pennies uneaten, traces of coffee and spicy dust

still hanging in the air, when her head shakes in sorrow as that dust
settles around her—even as she helps me load the vacuum,
heavy, pregnant, still warm in its belly, into my rusty two-door
Pinto in the fading light, pitying me even my car, even if the spell
doesn't work this time, it gives off its own peculiar odor, magic: I sweep
off my hands, shake hers, doff my hat, look at the plastic map's web.

I think I'll take the southwest arm of my pregnant, promising web,
find other ladies' doors to charm open, other dusty carpets to sweep.
In a warmer vacuum, I can refine the inner workings of my spell.

Quiet Letters

Pornsak Pichetshote

Christopher Anil Lomchai had a peculiar run. When he hurried, his eight-year-old feet arched upward, lifting his heels to skim over the ground. The soles of his feet never firmly rested until he stopped moving. He didn't realize it until it was brought to his attention years later, but Christopher Anil Lomchai always ran on his toes. Tonight, however—or perhaps tomorrow morning, his bedside clock flashing a green 3:15 A.M.—those toes propelled him over plush condominium carpeting. Chris was searching for a pen.

His uncle's apartment was a standard two-bedroom condominium with duo bathrooms (one in the hall, the other attached to the master bedroom), a kitchen, living room, and a foyer. Not finding any pens in his room, Chris darted outside. His uncle's bedroom was out of the question. No matter how easygoing Uncle seemed to be, it would be pushing congeniality too far to wake him up at 3:15 A.M.

The foyer—a parquet wood floor that connected the living room, hallway, and kitchen—had become the dining room in the two months since Chris moved in. A table was pushed up against the far wall, serving the triple use of dining table, work desk, or both simultaneously. Tonight it had been the latter. Dishes, bowls, and glasses sat in a sea of papers in alternating pink, yellow, and white. No pen.

Chris's arched feet brought him to the living room, also engulfed by a paper ocean. Crunching noises and rustling whips punctuated his search, as he checked between the cushions of the couch, around the videotapes stacked atop the television, and underneath the newspapers covering the coffee table and floor. Still no pen. Running out of rooms, he went back, toes returning to the dining room, and passing through it, to the kitchen. Hinges creaked between wooden collisions. He opened and shut drawers and cabinets, until there, inexplicably buried in a mound of silverware, was a pencil.

Boulevards of black magpies bridging roads of black ebony. Black-lit Christmas ribbon that sprawled throughout the sand like jumbled desert highways. No, no, that wasn't how the dream had started. Chris had recognized himself in his dream: clunky glasses, short legs, "Chinese eyes" like Dad's and "Indian hair" like Mom's.

He was standing on a crystalline floor when suddenly, out of the crystal, grew a transparent city. . . . Now, he remembered. Pen in hand, Chris sat on the cool kitchen floor and began his letter to his father.

พ่อครับ,

ตั้งแต่มาถึง America ผมเริ่มฝันมากขึ้นตั้งเยอะเลย มากกว่าอยู่ในเมืองไทยอีก! มีฝัน ๆ หนึ่งที่ฝันมากกว่าอันอื่น (จริง ๆ แล้วผมเพิ่งตื่นมาจากฝัน ๆ เลย) Chris คิดว่าถ้าหากกว่าเล่าให้พ่อฟังอาจจะช่วยเปิดหูเปิดตา Chris เองว่ามีความหมายหรือไม่ แล้วถ้าหากเล่าให้พ่อฟังแล้วพ่ออาจจะมี idea มากกว่า Chris

ในฝัน, ผมรู้สึกตัวอยู่ในเมืองประหลาด/แต่จริงๆแล้ว,ตอนแรกๆไม่เชิงว่าเป็นเมือง แต่เป็นพื้นกระจกแก้วแล้วพออยู่ยืนบนพื้นออกจากนั้นจะขึ้นตึกซึ่งทำไปโดยแก้วเหมือนกับพื้นรอบ ๆ ตัวอธิบายแล้วมันฟังเหมือนหนังหรือ TV คิด ๆ แล้วเหมือนหนัง Disney ที่ Chris กับ Uncle ดูบนโทรทัศน์, ไม่แน่ใจเหมือนกัน (แต่จริง ๆ แล้วทั้งคู่ก็มีลักษณะที่พวก America เรียกว่า fantasy)

พอตึกแก้ว

The dream-inspired words wrote themselves nimbly in a fluid cursive. It wasn't until two paragraphs later that Chris abruptly stopped. Looking at what he had written, he promptly crumpled the paper into a ball.

"Shit!" he said in an accent that turned a short *i* into a long *e*. *English. Not Thai.* His letters had to be written in *English.* Starting again, he tried to remember how letters in English started, with their carefully spaced words and peculiar grammar. His answer: the same way Thai letters did.

Dad sir,

Today had been cold, even if it was only October. The temperature had gone down to forty-five degrees, and his newly made schoolfriends had warned him that New Jersey would only get more frigid.

Two months ago, the sun was powerful and hot; then, it had been nice to know that although there were so many differences between Thailand and America, the weather wasn't one of them. Those same two months ago, Uncle had arrived to meet him at the airport. When Chris exchanged his first greetings with the cold Jersey climate, it hadn't occurred to him that everything would get so much colder so much faster. But of course it—and everything else in his new home— quickly changed. In those two months, his uncle's home for one turned into a condo for two. He had become "the newest classmate to the Emerson Elementary School second grade class." He'd made some friends, John and Peter, two Korean twins who spoke perfect English, and Johanna, an American girl who just moved from New York. His uncle had taken him shopping, and the boy of mixed Thai and Indian descent tried on and was bought his first sweater. Then, of course, there was TV. There was lots and lots of TV. *Different Strokes. Smurfs. Snorks. Facts of Life. He-Man* and *She-Ra.* America was in the details, and he had to tell Dad all about America.

Returning to his letter, Chris carefully arranged the blank papers on the kitchen floor, making a row of white windows that interrupted the kitchen tile's yellow patterns. Chris pictured how each sheet would fill with everything he wanted to say, black ink running until the white paper bled gray. There were all the things he had to tell, all the questions he wanted to ask: Were things good in Thailand? Did Dad still work long hours? Did he still read even though Chris was gone? It was okay if he didn't.

And as he always did when he thought of letters and envelopes, he cautiously wondered how it would be one day when he and his father would sit huddled around an orange fire in their backyard, burning this letter together as they had so many others. And after the papers grew gold, and then brown, and then curled, he wondered which of his words-to-be would be left uncharred.

First, though, he had to tell Dad about his dream.

Dad sir,
I have a dream this day. It was of

Dad sir,
I have dreams these days. It was of

Dad sir,
   I have a dream these days. It was of

Dad sir,
   I has dream one day. It was of

(Dad never had dreams. He remembered the night his mother confided that to him. He couldn't understand how it was possible that someone could never dream while he slept. It was true, his mother insisted. There were nights Dad woke up from a seemingly sound slumber to get up, walk about, and stare out the window. His mother explained how, on those nights, Dad stretched his stare out into the city, as if noticing a blotch of black in the night sky darker than the rest. He stared at it inquisitively, until she rose out of bed too. She draped her arms around him, and, each and every time it happened, asked if he was having bad dreams. He always gruffly replied that he never dreamed. Not to worry. Everything was fine. Go back to sleep. And he continued staring out the window.

Dads could act really cuckoo sometimes, his mother laughed quietly.

But if he never had dreams, much less bad ones, why did Chris's mother always ask him if he did? His mother chuckled again in response. I don't know, she replied, I guess mothers can act pretty cuckoo sometimes, too. With that, she usually draped her arms around Chris, resting her cheek on his forehead as she stared off into her own private haven.)

Dad sir,
   Today, I had a dream. It was about glass cities.

There. That seemed right.

Dad sir,
   Today, I had a dream. It was about glass cities. Chris stood on floor glass in dream. From the floor grew city.

Thinking of his mother, Chris stopped writing and looked down again at the blank pages of his unwritten letter. In the same way letters hummed his father's phrases and projected the crackle of campfires, his mother's voice was also hidden between the lines.

It wasn't that long ago, after all, that Chris and his father burned letters together. Not any of their own mail, of course, but other people's. His family lived on the bottom floor of an apartment building that housed ten other families. Like most buildings in urban Bangkok, theirs stretched upward, not outward, and this particular building housed a family on each floor. Bangkok was a city with ears constantly awaiting the whispered excuse to expand. For such a place, their building had one of the rarest commodities to be found: a backyard. Hardly a grand expanse of land, the grass was green enough, and there was room for children to run around. It came complete with a surrounding stone wall and densely leafed mango trees for cool shade.

Of course, the inside of the building made up for the luxury outside. The floors constantly needed mopping; cockroaches, while never rampant, were accommodating neighbors; and most annoying of all (at least to Chris's father), there was no formal mail distribution for the tenants. No mailboxes, slots, folders, or holes. Just a bench by the entrance, where letters and envelopes were dumped in a heap. The families of the building got into the practice of sifting through that mound for their individual mail. For Chris's father, a man with an obsession for organization, such disarray was intolerable. Unable to bear it, he eventually sorted the envelopes and packages into small piles, arranging each on the bench for the family to whom it belonged. In time, the building's residents got used to their self-appointed mailman.

Organizing the mail was fine during the days when his father was still unemployed. When Chris's father got a new job working as a desk clerk at the hospital emergency ward, however, he no longer had time for any extra chores. Nevertheless, on late nights on his way in, he gathered those letters and envelopes that sat on the bench and brought them into the living room, where, completely exhausted, he fell asleep. What remained the next morning was a pile of unsorted mail in the living room that grew when the process was repeated the next day. As the weeks passed, the same neighbors who once complimented him for his generosity of service complained about the tardiness of their important parcels.

Chris's parents never argued in front of Chris. They contained all arguments within their bedroom, after their son was sent to bed. So it was all kept within that room whenever Chris's mother implored her husband to take things easier. It was silly for him to be doing the mail now, she said. He was entirely too busy. Besides, the neighbors knew how hard her husband worked. It was disgusting how obnoxious they were being. She cared too passionately to watch her husband be so unappreciated, and if they weren't going to offer that respect, well, to hell with them. Her husband was ashamed his wife couldn't understand why there was nothing wrong with working hard. Their neighbors were right to be concerned about what belonged to them. He needed to try harder. They argued about it the way they debated all their disagreements, shouts and belligerence replacing statements and coaxing. Despite their nights of draped arms and bad dreams that were never admitted, whenever they disagreed, they disagreed in stereo.

Chris knew that. For a son who wants them to, the walls can leak voices. Although his parents tried to argue on tiptoe, voices raised at one moment, only to be checked with muted phrases later, certain words did make it through the building's thick walls. His mother's yells were punctuated with phrases such as . . . stop taking responsibility for everyone . . . open up . . . let others help . . . Stop protecting everyone. His father's retorts always included . . . don't understand . . . you're a woman . . . think only of yourself . . . a man's honor . . . so self-absorbed.

Despite those arguments, Chris's father refused to concede. He continued to come into the apartment exhausted, a pool of mail swimming between his outstretched arms. The task left undone, Chris's mother took it upon herself to distribute the myriad envelopes in her husband's absence.

Dad sir,

Today, I had a dream. It was about glass cities. In dream I stood on floor glass. City grew from the floor.

But after his mother . . . vanished . . . , Chris and his father found the space that could barely hold three was much too large for two.

On the day it must have happened, there were some things that weren't veiled in ambiguity. The weather was surprisingly cool, almost wet. The day was a Thursday. The bus from school was not as congested as it usually was. The sun had set early. His mother was reading him a bedtime story, an old Thai folktale that involved ogres, princes, and trickery. The memory of the story was particularly vivid, because of how badly his mother had told it.

A day can be the same jigsaw as an argument. The fragments you know are stirred in with the words you don't. You taste all the stories you can mix, and you drink whatever tastes right.

Chris lay in bed, covered by a thin blanket. His mother pulled a chair up by his bedside. She read from the passages in the story, her voice sliding between octaves: a steady, rhythmic tone for a narrator, a more excited, yet too feminine chord for a prince, and high squeaky voices for ogres. Ogres, of course, never spoke in high squeaky voices. When Dad told these stories, he had a knack for their sounds: low, guttural tremblings that reached out from the stomach. Mom could never get it right.

But then again, she wasn't supposed to. Dad was. During his days of unemployment, Chris's father took to reading his son a story every night. The ritual had been his idea. Chris chose a story each day. The name of the story was never told to anyone. Not even Chris's mother. As long as the book was just their secret—his father insisted—their time together was just their time.

To be honest, Chris had outgrown bedtime stories years ago, but there was something about the enthusiasm with which his father insisted that he should spend time every day reading a bedtime story to his son.

Unless he was arguing, Chris's father spoke in low, tired tones. His voice was lethargic for such a busy person, so it made no sense why that same voice would lend itself to storytelling, but it did. In just-their-time, with all the lights off but one, the door closed tight, and just Chris and his father, his father's voice shook off its sluggishness. He hurled himself into each story Chris chose, providing a voice for every character, a verbal deviance for every creature. Witches had sharp cackles. Dynamic youthful chords for princes. Low, trembling sounds for ogres. With his father's voice, Chris could forget he had outgrown bedtime stories.

Without that voice, he was wearing a ritual two sizes too small. His mother couldn't see that. When his father finally found his new job, she insisted that nothing needed to change. Despite Chris's refusals and protests, she came in to read to him every night, providing pip-squeaking screeches instead of sinister ogre growls. Every night, Chris told his mother she didn't need to; he was too old for bedtime stories. And every night, Chris's mother insisted. On the nights he was truly exhausted, Chris, exasperated, would yell and scream. Once, he even threw a book at her.

The night before the vanishing had been such a storytelling night. On that night, the walls again leaked voices. Loud shouts this time. His father was back from work extra late. His mother was shouting. Demanding. His father began shouting back. More shouting. A crash.

In his dark room, Chris listened for more sounds: more shouts, the slamming of doors. Chris was used to their fragmented arguments, but those fights had never been accompanied by so many other noises. He thought about leaving his bed, opening his door, and poking his head out, but in bed he stayed.

In the morning his mother was gone. His father told him she needed to go out for a night. She would be back the next day. He said no other words on the subject. When she didn't return after five days, his father's anxiety grew. As five days became seven, his father broke his wall of silence. On an arid summer day, with a voice calm and concise, he told Chris he was worried about where Mom was, but he was looking for her now. Don't worry; she'd be home soon.

Two weeks later, she still hadn't returned.

Dad sir,

Today, I had a dream. It was about glass cities. In dream, I stood on floor glass. From the floor grew city.

It was like wrestling water. He watched, as his father asked his wife's friends for new information. Any answers he received, however, he kept to himself. Questions regarding a missing mother were dodged. At times, the dodge came in a tired, exhausted tone. At others, it held a sharp edge that intimidated. Chris wrestled with liquid facts, until he grew frustrated and numb. When that numbness reached its climax, it became a voice, the high squeaky voice of ogres. That voice lingered and looped, until it became two tangible facts: He had thrown a book at his mother. His mother was gone.

On one of those nights, he made his way out into the living room. The lights had been shut off, leaving the room dark aside from the moonlight that slid in through the windows. It landed on the pile of mail his father still brought in each day after work. Before, his mother had distributed the mail when his father failed to, or she had moved it into a corner out of the way. Now, the plethora of parcels, envelopes, newsletters, and magazines sat in the center of the room.

Chris's father still believed he could distribute all the white and yellow envelopes, even with his mother nowhere to be found. His mother, despite her protests and cries of indignation, still distributed the mail when her husband couldn't. The whole building knew that his mother was gone, and yet there was still the obnoxious demands for letters to be delivered on time.

Chris imagined kicking the pile for spite, sending the envelopes hurtling through the air, and spinning back to the ground like leaves. But he was his father's son, and instead of a kick, he remained calm and composed, staring at the pile. Then, he went to it, sat down, and began to organize the heap into small mounds.

The large mail went first. The bulky manila envelopes. The newsletters and magazines. The brown-paper parcels. He surrounded himself with letters, a chaotic pile at his back, and it passed through him to its appropriate position in the ten-point semicircle before him, one for each family in the building. When he finished the larger mail, he moved on to the smaller envelopes.

As he reached out for the first white letter, he heard his father's footsteps behind him. He had watched his son from the hallway, silently staring at the sight of him in the dark room, knee-deep in a pool of mail and moonlight.

"ไม่ต้องลูก, ลูกไม่ต้อง" he said, shaking his head from side to side for emphasis. He threw the mail into a large black garbage bag he had retrieved from the kitchen. When he finished, he made his way to the door, to place the letters and envelopes back on the bench. He opened the door and paused. Chris watched his father, standing in the doorway, a rectangle of light rushing from the hallway to join the moonlight in the living room. His father looked over toward the bench by the front door, looked down at the black garbage bag in his hands, peered up the stairs toward the apartment overhead, and glanced back at the bag. He turned around abruptly, shutting the door, and told his son to follow him. They went out through the back.

The rusty hinges of the back door made a rapid squeal, as he led Chris outside. Quickly, they walked over to a dark corner of the back lawn, almost completely obscured by the two densely leafed mango trees that lurched over it. His father dumped out all the contents of the bag. He told Chris to sit down. As Chris folded his legs, his father told him about how, when he was reckless and stupid and young, he used to burn leaves with a magnifying glass. It's all right to do stupid things sometimes, as long as no one knows.

With that, he drew out a book of matches from his pocket and began to set tiny embers and twigs afire. It was the weakest of flames, but as Chris silently watched, his father grabbed a fistful of letters and gently threw them atop the tiny orange glow. The white paper wilted instantly, and the fire grew. Chris's father threw in more mail. The flames grew, and Chris watched, as white envelopes grew gold and then brown and then curled. Then, right before they could crumple into black, his father threw sand on them. He threw fifteen letters into that fire, tossing sand on them all before they crumpled into small black patches.

From those patches came the biggest pieces of those burned letters, and, in that voice that made ogres sound low and trembling, he read what he could of them aloud. It became a game. He read them, and sometimes Chris read them, and they filled in the charred blanks, pretending they were the people who had sent those letters. And they were them. They were happy like them or sad like them or grieving like them or mad like them. It was a game of make-believe, and although his father still made no mention of his mother, he was reading to his son again.

When they were done, they dumped the leftover mail onto the bench from where it had originally come. It sat there for the other tenants to finally pick up on their own. But every now and then, they'd do it again. Sometimes not for weeks at a time, but occasionally, Chris found his father sitting in the living room chair, staring out toward a pinprick of light that beamed in from far outside their windows. This led his father out through the front, to take anywhere from a handful to a small sackful of mail. The two spent the night sitting around a small yellow campfire, watching as the envelopes grew gold and then brown and then curled. And Chris's father read him a letter.

Dad sir,

Today, I had a dream. It was about glass cities. In dream, I stood on floor glass. The city grew out from the floor.

Those sentences still weren't right. They sounded funny. It seemed like he had gone through every possible combination of those words. *Sometimes the right answer just sounds right,* his English teacher had said. *Just repeat the sentence in your head, and put down what sounds right.*

Chris absently tugged at his dark brown hair. He silently repeated the sentences. They had to sound right.

Dad sir,

Today, I had a dream. It was about glass cities. In my dream, I stood on floor glass, and the city grew out from the floor.

Rice. Vegetable curry. Baked chicken. Dessert was coconut ice cream. Coke was drunk from tall plastic glasses. The announcement was made over dinner, one his father spent all evening preparing. During the meal, his father asked him about school, his health, followed by more school inquiries. By the time the announcement was made, it was time for dessert.

With his father already working long hours during the days, Chris was spending too much time at home alone. The hospital was now under a budget cut. His father was needed to work evenings and nights, or else the hospital would hire someone who could. The solution? Dad had a brother-in-law who lived in New Jersey who offered to take care of the boy in the States, at least until something settled. Between Chris and work, something had to be sacrificed. Chris was to be sent to stay with his uncle, at least until Dad could work something out.

His father brought the topic up slowly, cautiously, in his usual calm, stoic voice. He told his son how easy it was for children at a young age to learn new languages. Being immersed in a new envi-

211

ronment was different, but it would force him to learn the language quicker. Although it had been a while since his father had seen his uncle, he was a good man; he would take care of Chris. Everything would work out, and then eventually Chris would come back home once Dad settled everything out here in Thailand.

Chris told his father he knew. A phone call he had overheard a week ago had prepared him for the news.

His father's speech quickened. Everything was going to be all right. Whatever money he made, he would send part of it to America, to help with expenses. If there was a way they both could stay, he should know that his father would do whatever he could to find it. He was Chris's father, he knew what was best. Chris had to believe that.

His father gave him statistics about the number of parents who sent their children for schooling abroad. Then came more statistics about how much easier it was to find a job in Thailand if a person had some kind of international education. He referred to an article he had read comparing the two systems of education.

He explained how his own mistake had been not to learn any other languages besides Thai. His son had to learn from his mistakes. He had to be better than him. He was sorry about moving Chris. He was sorry about making his mother leave. He was sorry he didn't have a better job.

At the mention of his mother, Chris's mouth instinctively opened. He felt his tongue get wet, glands in the back of his mouth salivating, waiting to be formed into words. He raised his eyes from the dessert he had been staring at—the coconut ice cream that had been melting in front of him—and watched as his father spoke faster.

But Dad would help Chris be better than he was, his father explained. First, it would start with languages. Being in America, Chris would learn English, and be fluent in both languages. He'd write home every week—no, not every week, because that would cut in on school time, but every two weeks—and each time the letter would be in English, to make his Dad proud and show how successful his son was at learning this new language. Dad was sorry for making so many mistakes, but everything would be better now. His father stared down at the table, as he mumbled the next words, Dad was so sorry for everything.

Chris's mouth slowly closed. He and his father sat at the table in silence. Soon, his father reached out to the bowl of ice cream that sat in front of him. Carefully lifting the silver spoon to his left, he began eating.

The two ate in silence, before his father muttered something else: . . . I don't know where she is . . . *no one* knows where she is. . . . They think she's . . .

The silence continued, except for the clink of silver spoons meeting porcelain bowls.

Dear Dad,

Today, I had a dream. It was about glass cities. In my dream, I stood on a floor of glass, and the city grew out from the floor.

There. There, that had to be right.

Chris put his pen down to check his grammar one last time. It was correct. He was sure. Now . . . now, he'd just have to remember what else the dream was about. He closed his eyes, but all he could see was a huge blankness in his mind where the dream should have been. He couldn't remember what it was about. Feathers? Birds? Why was there a glass city? What happened next?

He figured how long it had taken him to write the first four sentences. Of course there were a lot of things he wanted to tell Dad, but Chris wrote slowly, and he couldn't write forever. He had to pick and choose what was important and what was not. Once picked, he had to stick to those important things. There was still school to talk about. There were other portions of his new life. All the new friends he had made. His uncle, who sometimes acted like a bigger kid than Chris, always happy, always smiling. Or maybe ask Dad how he's doing? If he was still having problems with his กระเพาะ? But how do you say ลำไส้ใหญ่ in English? Or สุขภาพ? How do you say สุขภาพ?

◆ ◆ ◆

An hour and a half later, Chris finished his letter and returned to bed. He had school that morning and needed sleep. It was now six o'clock, and from his window he could see the sun's morning brush strokes.

In Thailand, where the time was twelve hours faster, his father would be leaving for work, starting an evening shift that wouldn't end until the following morning. His mother would be wherever she was, doing whatever it was she did now. If she could do anything. If she was all right.

In America, it was twelve hours after it was in Bangkok, and Chris could think about other things. Why did he never open the door when his parents began shouting? Why didn't he say anything to his father over dinner? Why hadn't he demanded answers?

Chris lay in bed, staring out the window. Outside, light somersaulted in a dance of reflections and sparkles as it careened off windowpanes and cascaded throughout the sky. Two rooms away, Chris's letter sat on the kitchen counter, bathing in some of those same rays. Finally, it was finished.

Dear Father,

How are you doing? School is fine here. Uncle is well. He is very happy. I have three new friends at school. How are things back home? I am fine. I like New Jersey a lot. I miss you.

From,
Chris

It Will Happen in a Car

Mahani Zubaidy

It will happen in a car. We will be driving along 620 or 71 because those are the scenic routes. We will be talking about dogs and land, saying words like golden retriever, property market, and good community.

We will stop at a gas station and the guy behind the cash register, who is white and has dirty fingernails, wears a shirt that is too tight at the waist, a button on his stomach about to pop just like his belly button right under must be straining. I tell him twenty on two while you clean the windscreen.

When I get back in sucking on apple juice, you finish a doughnut in three bites, place the coffee cup in the holder, and say, "Let's hit the road," as if we were going cross-country because that's the kind of thing you'd like to do while I wonder how much more road I can take (traveling along freeways in America makes me feel like a ball of clay rolling along a straight line—a little of me bleeds, hardens, and dries onto the tarmac until there's nothing left, when it is the moist earth I want to return to). When I die, in America my body will not touch soil but rot in a box. But I don't tell you this though you are my prince and I've promised you my life.

We will stop and look at the view, which you can't get enough of, but from the window because you don't really want to get out of the car. I will turn and look at the view through your window. I will see you in your dark blue shirt, your short-in-the-top-and-long-in-the-back hair, your cheeks puffed low in your face, your stomach growing, and it will occur to me that you look like a pregnant lizard.

Manny's Climb

Vince Gotera

"He looks just like a damn spider in a web!" It must have been Piggy Figone who said that. "A Flip spider!" We had all laughed—me, the Three Rons, Crazy Greg, and a couple of other kids—as we watched Manny climb the transmitter tower. Hanging by the tips of his fingers. Even now, more than twenty-five years later, I can still imagine what he must have felt like; just the week before Manny's climb, the Three Rons had made *me* scale that tower. I can still remember how it felt: the wind parting your hair like a cold hand, the tower creaking as it swayed, like the rivets were gonna pop off one by one as if you were Wile E. Coyote in a *Roadrunner* cartoon, and the sky all around you a deep blue fishbowl. Manny just kept inching, shinnying up. Filipino spider, indeed.

I'll never forget the day Manny—Emmanuel was his full given name—transferred to St. Alfred's in the sixth grade. Third week of school, a bright Indian-summer morning with just a hint of crispness in the air. A new kid was in the schoolyard, where we were all waiting for Sister Mary Michael, the principal, to come out and ring that huge handbell of hers, telling us to line up. "My name is Manny Mendoza," he was saying to one kid after another. "D'ya want me to eat this paper?" He would then hold up a piece of paper, shredded on one end, where it had been torn from one of those pocket-size spiral-bound notebooks. Of course, each one of us, when asked that question, said, "Yeah!" What else could a self-respecting, red-blooded American eleven-year-old say? Boy, did he gather a crowd of kids as he chewed up and swallowed piece after piece of paper. Kids were beginning to cheer, to egg him on. "Manny! Manny! Manny!" In fact, just as Sister Michael came out on the school steps with her bell, Manny's pad ran out, and he tore a chunk out of his brown lunch bag with his teeth.

Well, I didn't know what to think about this new kid. For five years, I had been the only Filipino kid in the class, and now Manny made two. But, Jeez, what a clown! Did I want to be associated with this guy? One thing about Manny, though, he knew how to dress. His St. Alfred School uniform—white shirt, brown "salt-and-pepper" corduroy pants, brown cardigan—was always impeccably cut. The rest of us always seemed rumpled and baggy in our uniforms next to Manny. His pants had been altered, form-fitted to a sixteenth of an inch outside what the nuns might deem too tight. And his pants—I tell you, this is hard to do with cords—his pants were always starch-ironed with folds like razor blades. His sweaters always had a blousy look, kind of like "poet shirts" in lingerie catalogs, billowing out slightly in the sleeves before the gather of the cuff, a whisper of fullness at the waist before the cummerbund-like tightness hugging the hips. His white short-sleeve shirts, too, were always professionally starched. By three-thirty in the afternoon, we would be limp as wilted cabbage, but Manny's collars would still be crisp as cardboard. And he wore imported Italian half-boots! The rest of us wore Kinney's wingtips, but his boots were what we could call, in a year or so, "Beatle boots"—coming to a chic, sleek, and trendy point at the toe. Man, that Manny was sharp!

Don't get me wrong, now, Manny was no sissy. He may have dressed like a dandy, but he was no slouch on the basketball court. Every day at lunch, the Three Rons would rule. That was Ron Johnson, a tall black kid who played center on our fourth-grade team; Ron Morse, a freckled and carrot-topped Irish boy with a short-man complex, who would fight anybody that looked at him the wrong way; and Geronimo Lee Wong, a sullen half-Chinese, half-Apache kid who had beaten up white Ron the second week of school in second grade to earn his slot. It occurs to me now that the Three Rons were like some kind of demographic slice of early 1960s San Francisco. Anyway, the Three Rons were the apex of the boys' social pyramid, and some of the girls rather liked the Rons' dashing ways, at least until Manny showed up with his Italian half-boots. So Manny had to prove himself that first day. Well, no, it couldn't have been the first day, because Manny was sent home right after lunch with a stomachache. In fact, he had thrown his lunch away (what there was left of the paper bag), because he just couldn't bring himself to eat anything. But anyway, Manny showed himself over the next few days to be a pretty decent point guard. He could dribble real fancy—between scissoring legs, pizzicato behind the back—and he could sink two out of three jump shots from the top of the key. Until now, though, I can't figure out how he kept those Italian half-boots shined throughout the day, but he always did.

Back at the tower, all I could see of Manny's boots were his soles, and they were just as worn as the bottoms of anybody else's shoes. In fact, it seemed like there was the beginning of a hole in the left sole, but he must have been thirty feet above us, so who knows? In any case, the pointed toes were coming in real handy as Manny slipped them into one acutely angled foothold after another, as diagonal braces crisscrossed in front of and around him. As I looked at him against the backdrop of drifting clouds, the tower seemed to ripple and shimmer, sway slightly like the tower of Pisa must, I imagined. Jeez, that was one climb I would never want to do again.

When white Ron, in the sixth grade, noticed that the rest of us were growing taller around him, and that he was fading back in the growth curve, becoming a runt, one might say though still no one dared to say it to his face, he and black Ron devised a series of tests by which the rest of us boys could prove our manhood. One was to jump off the top of Chinese Ron's stoop to the sidewalk. Now this wasn't a straight-down drop, some ten feet or so. That wouldn't have been sporting enough. No, you had to sail at a forty-five degree angle across the gravitational pull of the earth, about fifteen feet *over* the steps. And there wasn't much room at the top of the steps for a running start. You just had to stand there and take off, hoping your knees could take the shock when—and if—you hit the sidewalk and not the last step. I guess it was fortunate no one got more than a skinned knee or torn pants. There were twenty-one steps, I remember distinctly, and that split second while you were in the air seemed like forever. Then you would hit rock bottom. Piggy was the best at that free fall. Piggy wasn't fat; he just had a little upturned nose, and with a name like Figone, well, his nickname was a natural. Manny survived that test too, though he did scuff his right boot.

Another stunt black Ron devised was walking around and over the N Judah tunnel entrance. The N Judah was a streetcar line that went underground for a mile and a half, or thereabouts, and then surfaced to continue its way downtown. For a while, we had been jumping on the back of the streetcars, riding on the outside and making funny faces at the backs of passengers' heads. One time, Chinese Ron and Crazy Greg even rode the N Judah—again, on the outside, hanging on to the back window ledge—all the way through the tunnel. After they rode back, Crazy Greg—his full name was

Gregory Romanoff, a good Russian boy—was jumping around like Daffy Duck, he was so jazzed. Now that tunnel ride's something I *just* could not do. Black Ron couldn't do it either, so he proposed the tunnel walk.

The tunnel entrance was flanked by two sidewalks that climbed the hill above the tunnel; at the top, the sidewalks met and continued up. Next to the sidewalks was a four-foot-high concrete banister, maybe a foot or so wide with a fairly gentle incline, while at the top, where the sidewalks converged, a level segment, about forty feet across, formed the upper rim of the concrete wall that edged the tunnel archway. Black Ron's idea was to walk on the banister, an uphill climb of maybe a hundred feet, then across the straight edge above—a real tightrope act, since you'd look down past your feet at the rails glinting below, with an occasional rumbling streetcar to shake you up, literally as well as figuratively—and finally downhill on the other side. White Ron and I, both small and fleet of foot, were the best at this stunt. Manny passed this test, too; in fact, he stood on one leg in the middle of the level crossing, and mimicked a statue of Mercury perched on one winged foot. "Look at me, you guys! No hands!"

Manny was getting close to the top of the tower now. He had been climbing for a solid seven minutes. With a couple of shaky transitions, I must say. I particularly remember that loose strut he encountered some ten feet earlier. Well, not exactly loose, since the rivets on either end were still holding. The strut would nevertheless quiver and rattle if you touched it, and you sure didn't dare put your weight on it. When I had climbed the tower the week before, I had looked down as I passed that strut, wanting to make sure I didn't put a foot on it. The view was magnificent. The Three Rons and the other kids were distant as ants. Crazy Greg's mouth gaped open. With sheer bravado born of adrenaline, I had leaned out over the abyss and yelled, "Hey, Crazy! You catching flies?" Boy, what a rush! The sun was shining, reflections glinting off the occasional shiny surfaces on the tower. Down below, on the other side of the tower from the kids, was Sutro Lake, also flashing reflections like you wouldn't believe. Well, not exactly a lake, more like a pond, really. It was beautiful.

Piggy and I went over to Manny's house one afternoon, after school. He had invited us to have cookies or something. His parents weren't home, but that was pretty common among us kids, all latchkey types. Manny lived in a typical San Francisco flat, a little dingy and dark, with most of the shades pulled down. All sorts of Filipino bric-a-brac all around: on the dining room wall hung a giant wooden fork and spoon, carved fancifully on the handles; also a black shield like an interstate sign, with miniature Moro swords and knives arrayed on it like inlaid stripes; in the corner of the living room, a hanging lamp festooned with a mobile of circular capiz-shell slices; and other touristy knickknacks. "Jesus H. Christ," Piggy said, laughing. "We're in the Philippines now."

"I can't help what family I was born into," Manny muttered, his eyes glowering as he turned on the tube. So anyway, Piggy and Manny and I were sitting in the living room munching on ginger snaps and watching Rocky and Bullwinkle, when Piggy's hand darted up into the air in front of his face. He had caught a fly. Not much to brag about, because that fly had clearly been in the house for a couple of days, and it was starting to slow down. Not yet at that stage where the fly becomes delirious and begins bumping into your face, but certainly not at the peak of condition either. After Piggy let the fly go, I reached out and grabbed it, too.

"Hey, watch this," I said, leading the way into the kitchen. Still holding the fly buzzing around inside my right fist, I asked Manny for a glass of water. He set it down on the counter, and I lowered my right hand into the water and let the fly go. "What do you think? Will he drown?"

"Sure," Piggy snorted. "He's a *Flip,* that fly!" Manny's lips were pressed into a firm straight line. The fly lay at the bottom of the glass, motionless, for quite a long time, maybe a minute, as we watched intently. And then I poured the water slowly into the sink.

"Now watch," I whispered. In the empty glass, the fly lay there for a moment and then seemed to shrug feebly. After a few seconds, he was on his feet, though a little shaky. In another half minute, he had recovered enough to sail into the air, buzzing as well as ever before.

"That's nothing," Manny said. He then snagged the fly in his palm, got it between finger and thumb. I remember how mad it was, buzzing and wriggling its legs. Then Manny popped it into his mouth and swallowed noisily. "There you go, Piggy," he said. "So much for your Filipino fly. I hate *everything* about the goddamn

Philippines." It was only at that moment that I realized how much Manny and I were in competition.

Manny was almost at the top of the tower now. He just had to reach his left upward and he would touch the base of the transmitter itself. That's as far as any one of us had ever gone. Just a momentary touch, to say you too had been there, had planted your flag at the North Pole, then back down to terra firma. Of course Manny went farther. Pretty soon he was standing on the transmitter base, swinging from the antenna itself like King Kong on top of the Empire State Building. "I'll be damned," black Ron said. "I thought that antenna would give you one hell of a shock." We all stood there with our mouths hanging open, like lightning was going to strike Manny any moment.

And then Manny turned to face the lake. He was just a silhouette up there, a figure cut sharply from the blue background of sky. Manny dove, kicking his legs to clear the chain-link fence around the bottom of the tower. In the air, Manny spread his arms like bird's wings. "Holy Mary," white Ron whispered, "Mother of God." In my head going on thirty years, in all our heads, I'm sure, though we never talked about it, Manny was dazzling as an eagle flashing in the heavens. None of us could tell at that moment if he was going to make it into the lake. I turned away, the image of Manny spread out against the sky indelibly burning in my brain.

Sports and Other Stuff

Anna Alves

"Where's your dad?" Connie Gallaway asks me, smiling at me with squinty, sun-hampered eyes. Connie is Carrie Gallaway's mom and is in charge of sodas this week. I like when she brings the drinks because she always gets Pepsi and Coke and 7Up and Mountain Dew. When it is our turn, we always bring Shasta sodas from Lucky's supermarket, which are not as good as the real thing, though I do like the grape. But it is always all gone by the time I get to the cooler. Everyone else likes the grape, too.

"He's around," I reply, shrugging, taking a big bite out of my stick of beef jerky.

"Tell him it's his turn for sodas next week," Connie says, still smiling, wiping the sweat from the back of her neck, smothered as it is by her big, bushy, blondish ponytail. I visually connect the dots on her freckled face as I nod and murmur my "okay."

All the Mom managers at the softball fields ask about my daddy because they think he is "so handsome!" Daddy does not look like all the other dads, pasty and pot-bellied, sprawled beneath the bleached blue summer sky with baseball hats crunched over balding or graying heads. Daddy is dark and wiry—smart as a whip and not afraid to express his opinions. Looks stern when he is not smiling and does sit-ups every morning and every night, tucking his toes beneath the couch and crunching his gut inward as he moves upward, crisp and efficient.

"Little girls are not supposed to play sports," Daddy had said when I asked him for permission to play.

The girls' softball league was holding sign-ups down the street at the just-named José Rizal Community Center. Saying nothing else, he concentrated on his breaths as he finished his sit-ups. Sitting cross-legged near his head, I drew spirals on my knees. After school that day, I went to sign up anyway. I used my allowance savings to pay the thirty-five-dollar entry fee. When Daddy found out later that week, he refused to drive me to any practices in his brand-new car.

Daddy drives a midnight blue Camaro, sleek and full of presence, just like Daddy, lean and sometimes mean, who plays pickup basketball at the playground courts, plucking steals from beneath the palms of tall lanky black boys more than half his age. Me and my two sisters always watched him perform superhuman skills, all round eyes. Daddy is short for basketball, but he is quick and tough, so the guys at the courts respect him. That is where he goes after a long day's work, so I used to ride my bike to practice before he came home. Mommy started driving me on the sly, in her shiny, silver, secondhand Volvo. I had been riding home in the dark.

Daddy followed us to the practice field one day. I guess he had come home earlier than usual. Mommy dropped me off, and Daddy must have stayed through practice because after, he met me at the edge of the practice field, took my arm, and led me to his car. He said nothing as we sat there in the dimming silence. I picked at my Rawlings leather mitt, pushing my finger in and out of the optional hole at the back. I wondered if I could play a whole game with my finger stuck out, just like that. It seemed kind of dangerous.

When Mommy finally drove up, he got out of his car to yell and scream at her, right there in the parking lot. Fortunately, my mommy is always really late, so everyone had already gone home. Too, her window was rolled down all the way because she had no air conditioning, so she could hear every word he said. Daddy screamed and yelled at me, too, so I would not be excluded, but I was farther away and had the air on with the windows up. I just kept my eyes down, staring at his sweaty gray T-shirt chest, running through the Wednesday night television schedule on ABC, Channel 13. First, *Eight Is Enough*, then *Charlie's Angels* and *Vegas* with Dan Tana. My sisters were sure to ask me since we did not subscribe to *TV Guide*.

But Daddy realized I was pretty good at softball, so I think the yelling and screaming was all for show. Just to make us remember that he had the final say. After that, he started driving me to practices, and even games, always saying that this was it, the only year I was going to play. After this year, no more. I am now in the middle of my third year and my two sisters are playing, too. And they are really pretty good as well.

My teams are always very talented, and this morning, we won the first game of our doubleheader, so we are now in first place all alone. My worries are twenty minutes away with the second game, not yet under way. So I sit back in a portable lawn chair in the shade of the old equipment shack, sipping a Pepsi and eating my jerky, waiting for that next game to start. Mommy's shiny silver Volvo is in the shop, so today she got to ride in Daddy's midnight blue Camaro. They are sitting in his car now because it is so hot out here. I lied when Connie Gallaway asked me where my Dad was because I did not want them to be disturbed.

Daddy has no use for fuss and is much too practical to be bothered with trivial details, especially when he is hunched over thick books with names like *Torts* or *Contracts* or *Constitutional Law.* My auntie, Daddy's sister who is a nurse, says it is because he is the oldest of twelve and worked the hardest to make a name for himself outside of their tiny province near Vigan, Ilocos Norte, in the Philippines. I do not know where that is on the world map hanging on my classroom wall and neither does my teacher, Mrs. Fields. We could not find it, even with the magnifying glass.

Mommy, on the other hand, grew up in the huge city of Manila, the daughter of a famous politician who was killed by a rival during a local election right when she turned sixteen. They renamed her street in Caloocan City after him, and that is where most of her family still lives. Mommy is all flutter and laughter, a butterfly doll with a huge crooked smile and twinkly brown velvet eyes. She likes to go to parties with cha-cha dancing and karaoke and most of all, enjoys *chismis* with big groups of other fluttery and laughing friends. Mommy is a food supervisor at Mather Air Force Base and works a lot, especially at night. She often looks tired when she comes home in the mornings, so I tell her to go straight to bed as I pour Fruit Loops into three plastic, kitty-poop-brown breakfast bowls for me and my sisters.

Sometimes I flip through her old photo albums just to see all the exotic places she has been. Mommy traveled the world after her graduation from the Philippine Womens' University and has pictures of herself with her friends, all facing three-quarters to the camera, the front foot turned just so, posing like friendly Pilipina fashion models with Jackie-O bouffants. She is bigger and more Mommy-looking now because she had us three girls, but she still looks good on the weekends when she turns gay and chic again for her friends.

I finish off the last of my beef jerky and then, I look over to see what my parents are doing in the Camaro. I watch them carefully.

Mommy and Daddy met on a blind date in a bowling alley in Manila. Mommy was visiting from New York City, America, where she had lived for two years as a "modern single woman." Daddy had just passed the bar exam after graduating from the University of the Philippines undergrad and law school. I've seen black-and-white pictures of him, skinny, dark, and solemn, getting sworn in among a crowd of dark faces, ready to embark upon his brilliant law career. Mutual friends set them up that night, and six months later, they were man and wife.

"It was a good match for both of them," my auntie told me, when I asked her, out of curiosity, why they got married.

When I asked Mommy, she said, "Your daddy would come to my house and visit me under heavy chaperon. We were not even allowed to hold hands! He stole a kiss from me the night before our wedding when my *nanay* went outside to see why the dogs were barking so loud."

Turned out later it was one of Mommy's former suitors—a soon-to-be doctor—hovering outside for a last glance at the love of his life before she went off to live as another man's wife.

"How was the kiss?" I asked, really wanting to know. I had read books that described it as "seeing stars" or "feeling as if the earth moved."

"It was hard and fast and quite shocking!" she replied, fluttering a bit and then smiling.

"If you never even held hands until the day of the wedding and the kiss was so fast, how did you know you were in love with him?" I asked her then.

"It was when a big earthquake hit Manila and your daddy called me right after from his office building miles away," she told me, her eyes soft. "He was so worried and kept asking me if I was okay. And he was calling from underneath his desk! I knew then that he cared. He had not thought of calling anyone else but me. That's when I knew he was 'the one.'"

For me, that counted under the category of "feeling as if the earth moved" since it was, after all, an earthquake. After that, I wanted to ask Daddy how it all went, but I was afraid to. He never talked about such things, and it was a very long time ago. I had fantasies about their courtship, imagining my daddy as the tall, brooding stranger who whisked my butterfly Mommy away from her whirling parties and swarming suitors with a dark glance and kept her enthralled with his intense gaze. I wrote countless stories about their boundless love in the Superfriends-emblazoned notebooks I bought for school—the ones I should have written my homework in, but did not. I got all A's anyway.

I was eight when in the car one day, coming home from buying groceries, Mommy told me about the woman who came knocking on Daddy's office door selling raffle tickets for the grand Rizal Day Celebration of which she was crowned queen. She was all of twenty-two years old—a good, strong, healthy Ilocano girl with barely a high school diploma and a thick, heavy accent. Daddy liked her very much, Mommy said. I thought about Daddy's late nights at the office, picturing him bent over his beloved books, trying once again to pass that California bar exam. He failed again, you know, Mommy continued. He always fails. But the last test was many months ago. I remember staring at my M&M's melting colors all over my palms as she cried and cried and cried. That's when I decided to use my notebooks for homework instead. I suddenly got B's.

I am all of eleven now, an all-star shortstop in the girls' softball league, and my grades are back up, especially since I've started reading bigger books with longer words. I like the thickest books best. I also like staying long hours after softball practice, until it gets almost dark, to work on my reaction skills. "The way to catch a ball," Coach always says, "is to stay soft. If your glove is soft, the ball will not be hard." So I practice hard to always stay soft.

We have had games every weekend this summer, unless someone forfeits and cancels. One Saturday morning, not too long ago, my team did not have to play because of that very reason, so we had barbecue at the house—me, Mommy, and my two little sisters. Daddy came home and began yelling, so of course Mommy started crying. My sisters stayed outside, playing with six stray kittens nestled conveniently at the farthest corner of the backyard. I came in, put my hands over my ears, and ran out of the house. And I kept on running, all the way down the street and around all the corners.

Daddy caught up with me two blocks later in his shiny sportscar and drove me to Baskin-Robbins for a hot fudge over chocolate chip ice cream sundae. On a wooden bench at the public park, he put his face down into his hands, sobbing. "I tried to love your mommy," he choked out, "but I can't. I just can't." Daddy never cries. I stared into my sundae and made swirly with my pink plastic spoon as the late afternoon sun melted the iciness away, leaving me just with warm, gooey fluid. I ignored the stares of the kids at the playground and patted my daddy's shoulder saying, "It's all right, Daddy. It's all right."

But Mommy believes that divine intervention includes salvation of love stories gone wrong. She prays to the Holy Mother Mary in the middle of all the candles-in-glasses on the makeshift altar, atop the big old Zenith color TV in her room. She chants prayers at the giant wood-carved rosary hanging behind Mother Mary's lifelike figure. She thinks Daddy has had a spell cast over him by the beauty queen, and she is determined to find a way to counteract it. She talks to under-the-table *hilots* and bargain *babaylans* and tries a variety of methods from mild potions to incantations to burning pictures. And she waits—waits for the world to stop shaking again so that it will be as solid as her heart once more.

Coach suddenly yells at me, "C'mon! Hurry! We're gonna start!" It is time to play our second game

I toss my now-empty Pepsi can into a rusty metal garbage bin. Glove in hand, I start a trot toward diamond number one when Mommy suddenly laughs and Daddy does, too. I stop and stare at the blue Camaro. The passenger door is open, and, facing each other, Mommy and Daddy are bent over with laughter. I am struck dumb by the sight. Then, I remember that tomorrow, Mommy will have her Volvo back and tonight, after dropping all of us off, Daddy will go home to someone else. So I shrug and turn away, heading down to where my teammates await, in position between chalked regulation lines, taking my place at shortstop between second and third base, to field grounders and throw bullets from my arm at first.

Opossums and Thieving Pelicans

Paulino Lim Jr.

We home owners on our block, with a cul-de-sac on the south side of the street, are all members of Neighborhood Watch. We receive notices of meetings and monthly reports on crimes in the area from our block captain, Mrs. Rampling, a retired school teacher. With poise distilled from thousands of classroom hours, she presides at club meetings, organized to combat residential burglaries. Last summer we heard accounts of unusual thefts.

"Someone came and cleaned out my strawberry patch, darn it!" said Mrs. Sergeant, who works at the McDonnell Douglas aircraft plant nearby.

Others laughed, as I recalled a letter from my mother in the Philippines. She awoke one night and surprised a thief in the kitchen, stuffing his mouth with leftover rice. He ran away carrying the pot with him.

"Let me tell you," said Dagmar, called Brunhilda behind her back by those intimidated by her six-foot stature and platinum hair, "my next-door neighbor, who's Japanese, tells me that he's missing three koi fish from his backyard pond."

"What on earth is koi?" This came from garrulous Charlie, who lives across the street from my house; he's probably never heard of koi doctors in Beverly Hills, ichthyologists who treat ailing members of a species that can cost as much as five thousand dollars each.

"Oh, it looks like a giant goldfish."

My wife, Marta, who loves everything Japanese, turned her brown face toward me with a look that said we were going to have a good laugh later. Delaying reaction or postponing laughter, I know, perpetuates the myth of inscrutable Asians, who simply fear that a spontaneous expression might offend, or making a face might mean loss of face.

"He doesn't speak English very well," Dagmar said. "The other morning he says to me, 'Missy, missy, three koi fish gone from fish pond.'" I wanted to laugh, knowing how Charlie's wife mimics the German accent of Dagmar, whose "house" speech comes out a clipped "haus."

At least there were no burglaries, break-ins, or car thefts involving the sixteen homes of our block. The meeting at the park club-house soon turned to chat, the mystery of the missing strawberries and koi forgotten. Tony, a fireman, told the story of a Florida burglar alarm salesman who was caught breaking into a house. Apparently, the salesman would talk to homeowners, try to sell them alarms, and help undecided customers make up their minds by burglarizing their houses.

"Dagmar," Charlie said, "I get mixed up between your neighbor and that other Asian with the ugly olive tree in his front yard. Is he Korean?"

I often see him on a ladder, a brown grocery bag for a hat, trimming the olive tree that he has shaped into two globes.

"No, he's also Japanese."

"For a Japanese he sure is a lousy gardener. I swear that tree looks like his balls."

Everyone laughed. Two worlds or two balls; the genitalia allusion was the funnier joke. We all like Charlie; he speaks his mind and drinks his Scotch with gusto. The first time our house needed painting he asked me, "Have you seen the Filipino houses on Magellan Street on the next tract?"

Who hadn't seen them and snickered? Three boldly painted houses in a lower-middle-class tract of boxlike units with single garages. Pinks, apple greens, and scarlet reds. The pink house had pink wrought iron fence, potted cactus, and two stone flamingos.

He probably wanted me to say, "Gaudy, aren't they?" Instead I blurted, "As a matter of fact, Charlie, I'm planning to strip my house of its gray and white and repaint with chartreuse and fuchsia. What do you think?"

He left in a huff. Recent Filipino immigrants gained the reputation for ostentatious exterior decor of their tract homes. I first heard about it when I worked for the U.S. Navy; I served my twenty years and applied for citizenship upon my retirement. Even my barber, who is gay, recently told me of his Filipino neighbor who painted the wood trim orange and raspberry red.

The mystery of the missing strawberries was solved two days after the meeting at the clubhouse. I was sitting at the bar watching Marta chop onions and slice potatoes and oranges—the stuffing for the two wild ducks marinating in Chablis.

"I need onions for the sauce," she said. "Could you get two more?"

Flashlight in hand, I slipped out the patio door to the vegetable garden we plant each summer in an area of about forty square feet. I pulled out two onion bulbs the size of billiard balls, stripped the outer layers from the dried leaves down to the roots.

A rustle, a hiss. I flashed the beam on the eggplants, stringbeans, and a hairy animal eating tomatoes. A pig! It had a white pointy face and naked tail, its pelage gray and dirty-looking.

"Marta," I called from the patio, "come out here quick! There's something I want you to look at."

Through the glass door I watched Marta walk from the kitchen light, a knife in her hand, until her five-foot frame became a silhouette at the doorway. I often wonder how the missionaries react, Mormons and Jehovah's Witnesses, when they knock on our door and see this long-haired petite Filipina with a kitchen knife in hand, saying, "Yes?" She once warned me that I should never surprise her at night, when I come from out of town, and showed me a cleaver she keeps under the bed.

I flashed the light on the animal, its tail wiggling in the dark like a giant earthworm. It hissed and squirmed its way through the tomato vines.

"It's an opossum."

"I thought for a moment it was a pig. I've never seen an opossum before."

"I have, at the nature center on the other side of the river. That's probably where it came from."

The river separates Los Angeles from Orange County in the suburb of Long Beach, where we live; on the other side is Seal Beach. The water comes from the mountain, sewage lines and irrigation spills, so perhaps it can be called a river. From the county's point of view it is a flood-control canal that empties into the sea. Levees protect both sides, rising fifteen feet above the ground, leveled and asphalted at the top for joggers and cyclists.

"You know," Marta said, brandishing the knife, "we could make a stew with that opossum."

She wasn't kidding; she grew up on a farm and helped slaughter pigs and goats. I kept the light on the opossum as it grasped the cypress and pulled its stout body up the branches, with the aid of its prehensile tail.

"I had an interesting visit to the nature center with a bunch of Girl Scouts," Marta said, back in the kitchen. "We learned that about one hundred opossums live in that preserve. Many escape and look for food elsewhere."

"We should call the nature center and ask them what to do."

"How about opossum stew with potatoes, okra, and red pepper?"

"Hurry up with that wild duck. I'm getting hungry."

A woman from animal control of the city of Long Beach came with a trap, a wood frame covered with wire mesh, three feet long, sixteen inches wide, and eighteen inches high. She raised the door and showed us where to put the bait on the opposite end, a wallet-size piece of wood attached to a tripping mechanism. She left a can of catfood to use as bait.

Two weeks later, a meeting of the Neighborhood Watch of the tract was called. More than one hundred home owners showed up. The woman chairing the meeting introduced herself as the victim of two burglaries and recited known facts. The screwdriver was the basic tool of a burglar; it took three minutes for a residence to be robbed. Two daytime robberies had occurred; thieves using trucks disguised as movers hauled away furniture, stereos, and VCRs.

The councilman representing the district took the floor; he was tall, white-haired, and prepared to listen patiently to complaints. I winced when a woman said, "There's been an influx of foreigners on our tract, coming here to fish on the river."

On sunny weekends the river becomes a play area for two kinds of sports, waterskiing and fishing. The boaters and skiers are invariably white, the fishermen members of ethnic minorities. Motorboats scatter seagulls and fishermen reel in their lines as the skiers splay the water.

African Americans cast their lines from the levees close to the Alamitos Edison plants that pour steaming water into the river; Spanish Americans stay upriver; and Asians, mostly Vietnamese, go farther up where the water is shallow and grass grows. Some bring children with them and leave trash behind, styrofoam cups, plates, and bottles.

"It's awful, all that garbage," said Tony. "It takes a good rain to wash it down the river to the ocean."

"We should block off the street close to the freeway."

"Well, if we did that," said the councilman, "it would take longer for fire trucks and ambulances to get to this tract in an emergency."

"About two years ago, helicopters used to fly above with loud-speakers warning pseople not to fish in the river."

"Well, the council decided that cops had more important things to do. Besides it was costing the city two hundred dollars an hour to fly a helicopter."

"We could get the city to put up 'No Parking' and 'No Fishing' signs."

"That can be done."

"How soon can we get the signs put up?"

"We have to go through an ordinance procedure. First of all, you folks have to sign a petition."

We had quite a success with an earlier petition. An agency taking care of a group of young men and women on a drug rehabilitation program got permission to use the park and clubhouse during weekdays. The residents complained that the inmates were not properly supervised and kept their children away from the park. Tennis buffs reported that the inmates threw firecrackers that exploded on the court as they played.

The meeting broke up into small groups; our block members gathered in one corner. Mrs. Sargent reported that she had seen the opossum eating strawberries, and Dagmar said her Japanese neighbor woke up early one morning and found pelicans perched on the fence looking down on his pond.

"He thinks the pelicans are eating his koi."

It began to make sense. Pelicans and seagulls, driven from the river by water-skiers and fishermen, searched for food elsewhere and found it in people's backyards. A few nights after that meeting, we were watching television when I heard the trapdoor shut. Marta had replaced the catfood bait with a slice of corned beef we had on St. Patrick's Day.

"Marta," I said, "I think we got him"

I grabbed the flashlight and we went out to the garden. Inside the trap the opossum turned its pink nose and beady black eyes to the light, bristled the stiff hair on its face, then continued chewing on the corned beef.

"Well," Marta said, "here's our chance to experience what's considered a delicacy in some parts of the country."

Standing close to the trap, I smelled something fetid and musky, like the foul odor of a kitchen knife that was used to cut fish and left unwashed for days.

"I already found a Cajun recipe for roast opossum."

"I don't know about that—"

"God, what's that smell?" Marta cried, pinching her nose.

I waved the flashlight at the trap.

"Let's call animal control," Marta said, quickly turning away.

Scavenging on Double Bluff

Shirley Geok-lin Lim

I
My children call these wish-stones, Anne said,
studying the warm brown quartz
I had picked with its perfect elongated
white circle; when that circle is
unbroken, that's what makes them wishes.
I wished she had not told me this.
All week I thought of getting another
down by Double Bluff Beach.
This afternoon I take the time to bike
and walk. Some of us can pick up unbroken
spindles where others see only fragments
and shell bits; can gather a dozen
in a minute, whole and bleached.
Rocks lie everywhere on mud flats.
Serpentine, granite, sandstone, calcite,
agate: igneous and sedimentary,
names enough to fill my pockets.
I find the colors, lines, and shapes
as I find spindles in the shore litter.
Starving at six makes one grow up sharp
at scavenging, and I have seen
strangers turn dubious at my luck.
My eyes stoop to the search.
I do not stop for the blue herons
Or the far islands and inlets. The heron
hunts with me, hour after hour,
although I no longer know what it is
I wish for: love, money, position,
picked up like these shells and stones
that weigh down my backpack.

II

What is the difference between
having nothing and too much?
"You have too much," one complimented,
then asked for my things. But that's beside
the point. It's the work of finding
gives them meaning—work of a mind
honed for surviving. The Chinese,
as I found in Shanghai, at the garden
of the Minor Administrator, prefer
edges of unequally worn stone,
spying buttes, peaks, crags, and scarps
lift up against wear and centuries.
I must have never been Chinese.
I like my rocks smooth and worn
through millennia of water, storm, and tide;
round as the round of loaves; circles
of breasts hurting with milk
on round pillows; as a lunar month finds
an open Oh!, a yellow wheel;
round scrotum swollen at touch.
Complete as unbroken bands
of color, stones that are wishes.
I scavenge dandelion leaves, chicory,
wild onions, beach plums, thimbleberries.
I'm scavenging in case of a famine,
in case I'll have to go hungry,
wishes worn smooth, worn daily,
in my round mouth, my anxious hand.

Seaweeds

Shirley Geok-lin Lim

This is the farthest out in the Sound I'll ever be,
the ebb tide so low I've walked a quarter mile
of sand flats rippling on and on like washboards
laid end to end. The waves are puppies rolling
over, lapping with blind eyes, gentle
and tender. You forget how large they'll grow,
how sloppy and brutal they can be. Like gardens,
the seaweeds wash to and fro, shining clean
you can almost taste them fresh rinsed
in your mouth. As many greens as on this shore:
lettuce green, early asparagus, dark steamed
artichoke, a bracken glow as if sea
water grows colors brighter than air. I wonder
about the mermaid child who'd wanted the world
in air and stone, who'd left her bull kelp forests,
golden climbers, swollen purple pods
for the raw rough bark of conifers and eucalyptus.
Weeds is not what I would call these limpid grasses
and broad dulses. Sugar wrack, grapestone, bulbous
and tufted, stringy, tubular, streamers,
fungiform, multiform, a sea diversity
as lavish as on land. But I cannot walk
these flats endlessly. I must turn back
and face the new houses built to look out
to the Pacific. I have counted twelve flags
streaming on the late August air drafts,
a thirteenth almost too small for myopic eyes
to note in the distance, and who knows how many
more, flags that flap or hang or fly, forbidding
and uniform. Seaweeds, green and brown, gripping
onto their holdfasts of shell and stone,
drift slowly, wave with the incoming tide.
Today I have said good-bye to my son,
let him go onto this shore of flags and gardens.

236

Contributors

Noel Alumit wrote the play *Mr. and Mrs. Laquesta Go Dancing*, which was produced by Teatro Ng Tanan in San Francisco. His one-man show *The Rice Room: Scenes from a Bar* is currently touring. He received an Emerging Voices fellowship from PEN Center USA West and a Community Access Scholarship to UCLA's Writers Program to develop his first novel, *Letters to Montgomery Clift*. Noel would like to thank Hope Edelman for teaching him the essay form.

Anna Alves is a Pilipina writer who enjoys expressing herself in many different forms: journalistic articles, creative stories, plays, and song lyrics. She also loves the San Francisco 49ers and thinks women athletes rule. Some of her work has previously appeared in *Pacific Ties*, the *Asian and Pacific Islander Newsmagazine at UCLA* and *Amerasia Journal*. Alves holds a master's degree in Asian American studies from UCLA and is currently working on her first novel.

Anh Quynh Bui is a Vietnamese American Ph.D. candidate in the Department of English at the University of California, Berkeley. She is currently working on a dissertation on sound in film.

Kim Ly Bui-Burton is a Vietnamese American poet and public librarian. Her work has appeared in several anthologies, including *I Am Becoming the Woman I've Wanted*, awarded the 1995 Before Columbus Foundation National Book Award, *Passionate Hearts: The Poetry of Sexual Love*, *Squaw Review*, and *Footwork: Paterson Literary Review*. She lives on the central coast of California, with her husband, four children, one dog, and one cat.

Nick Carbo is the author of a book of poetry *El Grupo McDonald's* and the editor of *Returning a Borrowed Tongue: An Anthology of Filipino and Filipino American Poetry*. Among his awards are fellowships in poetry from the National Endowment for the Arts and the New York Foundation for the Arts. Carbo is of Filipino and Spanish heritage.

Fiona Cheong was born in Singapore. She received her B.A. in English and M.F.A. in creative writing from Cornell University, and is currently an assistant professor of English at the University of Pittsburgh. She is the author of *The Scent of the Gods* and a contributor to *Charlie Chan Is Dead: An Anthology of Contemporary Asian American Fiction*. Cheong's second novel, *Shadow Theatre*, is currently in circulation. "Granddaughter" is from a work in progress.

Cheng Lok Chua was born in Singapore of Chinese parents and has been a resident of the United States since 1965. He is a professor of English at California State University, Fresno, having also taught English at the University of Singapore, the University of Michigan, and Moorhead State University, Minnesota; in addition, he has taught Asian American studies at the University of California at Santa Barbara and at UC Berkeley. His work has been published in the *Massachusetts Review, Symposium, MELUS, Revue des Lettres Modernes, Ethnic Groups,* and other periodicals.

Oliver de la Paz was born in Manila, Philippines, and raised in Ontario, Oregon. He has an M.F.A. in creative writing from Arizona State University and teaches English composition and creative writing. He has recently been published in the *Crab Orchard Review, Hayden's Ferry Review,* and the *Marlboro Review.* De la Paz currently shares a living space with Rosie the pug.

Lan Duong is currently studying comparative literature at the graduate level at the University of California, Irvine. She hopes to complete her doctorate soon and teach at a university, but mostly, she wants to continue poetry writing as much as possible (it keeps her sane). Lan is also published in *Watermark: Vietnamese American Poetry and Prose* and in the journals *dis•Orient* and *Crab Orchard Review: A Special Issue on Asian American Writing.*

LeAna B. Gloor was born LeAna Beth Ward Almoite in Baja California, Mexico. While living in Hilo, Hawaii, she compiled a series of poems relating to her Filipino heritage and the struggle for affirmation within a culture. She currently makes her home on the Olympic Peninsula in Washington State. Gloor's work has also appeared in the *Seattle Review* and the *Chaminade Literary Review.*

Eugene Gloria was born in Manila, Philippines, and was raised in San Francisco. He was educated at San Francisco State University, Miami University of Ohio, and the University of Oregon. His poems have appeared in such publications as *Parnassus: Poetry in Review, Madison Review,* the *Asian Pacific American Journal,* and recently in *Crab Orchard Review, Gulf Coast,* and *Willow Springs.* Gloria received a Fulbright fellowship in 1992, an artist grant from the San Francisco Arts Commission in 1995, 96 Inc.'s Bruce P. Rossley Literary Award, and the George Bogin Memorial Award from the Poetry Society of America. He was a scholar at the Bread Loaf Writers' Conference and a resident at the Vermont Studio Center, the Mary Anderson Center for the Arts, and the MacDowell Colony. Gloria currently teaches English at Holyoke Community College.

Poet and fiction writer **Elizabeth Gordon,** who received her master's degree in creative writing from Brown University, was born in Saigon (now Ho Chi Minh City) to Vietnamese and American parents. Her work has appeared in such publications as *Slant, Green Mountains Review, CutBank, Plainsong,* and *Home to Stay: Asian American Women's Fiction;* she also has written reviews for the *Prose Poem: An International Journal.* Gordon is working on her first collection of poetry, tentatively titled *Miscegenation.*

Vince Gotera teaches creative writing and multicultural literature at the University of Northern Iowa, where he serves as editor of the *North American Review.*

He has published two books: a poetry collection titled *Dragonfly* and a critical study, *Radical Visions: Poetry by Vietnam Veterans*. His fiction recently appeared in the anthology *Contemporary Fiction by Filipinos in America*. Gotera is listowner of the e-mail discussion list FLIPS, which focuses on Filipino literature and writing <flips@uni.edu>.

Aurora Harris was born in Detroit, Michigan, and is the daughter of a Filipino mother and African American father. She attended Wayne State University and teaches poetry in high schools, libraries, shelters, and juvenile facilities. Harris is the founder and program director of the World Voice Literary Series at the Graystone International Jazz Museum. Her publications include *Michigan Feminist Studies* number 12 (University of Michigan, 1998), *Brooding the Heartlands* (Bottom Dog Press, 1998), and *Seeds* (Sisters of Color, 1995, 1996, 1998).

Hanh Hoang was born in Vietnam in 1956 and grew up in Saigon. She attended Scripps College, New York University, and the Sorbonne, Paris. Ms. Hoang has worked as a freelance journalist for the *San Diego Union, Berkeley Voice,* and *Transpacific* magazine. She currently lives in northern California and is working on a novel, from which excerpts have appeared in Tristine Rainer's *Your Life as Story* (Putnam).

Minh-Mai Hoang is an editor for an Internet directory and the literary journal *Oyster Boy Review* (www.levee67.com). Her writing has appeared in the *Washington Post* and the *International Herald Tribune*. She now lives in Oakland, California, after spending 1995–1998 in Vietnam and South Africa.

Jade Quang Huynh was born in South Vietnam in 1957. His published work includes a memoir, *South Wind Changing,* and he served as coeditor of a collection titled *Deliverance by Sea: Vietnamese Boat People's Narratives* (forthcoming). He received a bachelor of arts degree from Bennington College in 1987. In 1992, he graduated from Brown University with a master of fine arts. He is a recipient of the National Endowment for the Arts. Huynh teaches at Appalachian State University.

Cuong H. Lam was born in Ca Mau, Vietnam. In 1980, he immigrated with his family to the United States. Lam graduated from the University of California, Berkeley, with a degree in Asian American studies and a minor in creative writing. His works have appeared in *hardboiled,* an Asian Pacific American newsmagazine he cofounded in Berkeley, and *Yolk* magazine. Lam currently lives in Los Angeles, California.

Joseph O. Legaspi was born and raised in Manila, Philippines, and immigrated with his family to Los Angeles in 1984. He holds degrees from Loyola Marymount University and the Graduate Creative Writing Program at New York University. Currently, he lives and works in New York City. His poems have appeared in the *Seneca Review, Many Mountains Moving, Poet Lore, Literary Review, Gulf Coast, Bamboo Ridge,* and *Hayden's Ferry Review,* among others.

Paulino Lim Jr. is a professor of English at California State University, Long Beach. He is the author of a scholarly monograph, *The Style of Lord Byron's Plays* (1973); an anthology, *Passion Summer and Other Stories* (1988); and a quartet of political novels: *Tiger Orchids on Mount Mayon* (1990), *Sparrows Don't Sing in the Philippines* (1994), *Requiem for a Rebel Priest* (1996), and *Ka Gaby, Nom de Guerre* (2000).

Shirley Geok-lin Lim's first collection of poems, *Crossing the Peninsula* (1980), received the Commonwealth Poetry Prize. She has published four volumes of poetry subsequently: *No Man's Grove* (1985); *Modern Secrets* (1989); *Monsoon History* (1994), which is a retrospective selection of her work; and *What the Fortune Teller Didn't Say* (1998). She was interviewed by Bill Moyers for a PBS special on American poetry, *Fooling with Words*, in 1999. She has also published three books of short stories and a memoir, *Among the White Moon Faces* (1996), which received the 1997 American Book Award. Lim's coedited anthology, *The Forbidden Stitch: An Asian American Women's Anthology* (1989), also received the American Book Award. She has published two critical studies, *Writing South East/Asia in English: Against the Grain* (1994), and *Nationalism and Literature: Writing in English from the Philippines and Singapore* (1993), and has edited or coedited three other volumes. She has three other edited or coedited volumes: *Transnational Asia Pacific* (University of Illinois Press), *Power, Race and Gender in Academe* (MLA Press), and *Asian American Literature: An Anthology* (NTC/Contemporary Publishers). She is Chair Professor of English at the University of Hong Kong, and professor of English and women's studies at the University of California, Santa Barbara.

Maria Antonette Mesina (Toni Mesina) graduated from the University of Hawaii at Manoa with bachelor's and master of arts degrees in English with interests in ethnic literature. She is a second-generation Filipina born and raised in Hawaii and is currently a religion teacher at Sacred Hearts Academy in Honolulu. Toni enjoys hula, volleyball, and the beach.

A graduate from the University of California at Davis, **Pos Moua** has studied with the poets Gary Snyder, Alan Williamson, and Sandra McPherson. Some of his short poems were published in Sacramento's *Poetry Now, UC Davis Poetry Review,* and *The National Library of Poetry.* His collection of poems, *Towards the World Where the Torches Are Burning,* is awaiting publication. Currently, he lives in Merced, California, with his wife, two sons, and two daughters, and teaches English and Hmong full-time at Merced High School and part-time at Merced Community College.

Sophie Nguyen was born in Washington, D.C., in 1967, at the height of the Vietnam War to an American mother and Vietnamese father. Nguyen has devoted herself to deconstructing Vietnamese-American relations and to understanding Vietnam's long history of resistance to colonization. Nguyen was formally trained as a visual artist and produces video and electronic artworks. Her recent videos explore her family members' changing emotional and political relationship with Vietnam, where Nguyen's father served as a government official of the Republic of South

Vietnam during the final years of the Vietnam War. For this reason, the author has taken the name "Nguyen" as a pseudonym to protect the identity of family members in both the United States and in Vietnam. "Famine All Around" is Nguyen's first work in a literary, nonvisual form.

U Sam Oeur was born in Cambodia in 1936. He received his M.F.A. from the Iowa Writers' Workshop in 1968, but returned home, where he was elected to the National Assembly and served as a UN delegate. He survived six different concentration camps under Pol Pot. U came back to the U.S. in 1992 and has received political asylum. His *Sacred Vows* was published by Coffee House Press in 1998 and his autobiography is forthcoming. He lives in Minneapolis.

Ruth Pe Palileo studied microbiology for years before falling asleep over her evolution textbook and writing her first poem when she woke. In troubadour tradition, she performed her poetry at various Chicago venues, both spoken versions and ones set to music. Equal parts brutal honesty and romper-room fun, her work blends Asian ideas with American rhythm and language. She has been published in such magazines as *Proteus Literary Magazine* and *New Works Review.*

Isabelle Thuy Pelaud is a graduate student of Vietnamese ancestry in ethnic studies at the University of California at Berkeley. She has been reading prose and poetry periodically throughout the Bay Area since 1993.

Anh Phuong-Nguyen has finished her undergraduate studies at Bryn Mawr College and is currently enrolled in the Master of Theological Studies program at Harvard Divinity School.

Pornsak Pichetshote is a second-generation Thai American who spent half his childhood in America and the other half in Thailand, where he and the language barrier became intimate friends. Currently, he lives in Boston. His nonfiction has appeared in such magazines as *Insider, Indy,* and *Subliminal Tattoos.* "Quiet Letters" is his first published fiction.

Jon Pineda's poetry has appeared in the *Asian Pacific American Journal, Crab Orchard Review, Hayden's Ferry Review, Poetry Northwest, Puerto del Sol,* and elsewhere. He lives in Norfolk, Virginia, with his wife.

M. G. Sorongon grew up in Saginaw, Michigan. She attended Vassar College and is currently enrolled in the M.F.A. program at the University of Alabama. She lives in Ojai, California, where she is at work on a collection of short stories and her vegetable garden.

Ira Sukrungruang is a second-generation Thai American born in Chicago. His nonfiction has appeared in *Crab Orchard Review.* He is pursuing an M.F.A. in creative nonfiction at the Ohio State University.

Geronimo G. Tagatac is a first-generation Filipino American. His father was born in Ilocos Norte, in the Philippines. His mother was a Russian Jew, and his step-mother is a Cajun from Happy Jack, Louisiana. Tagatac is a Vietnam veteran. He has published stories in *Writers Forum*, the *Northwest Review, MoonRabbit Review, River Oak Review, Orion, El Locofoco, Mississippi Mud,* and *Alternatives*. He lives and writes in Salem, Oregon.

BeeBee Tan-Beck, a Malaysian-born Chinese immigrant and graduate of the University of Washington, Seattle, has been published in various magazines such as *13th Moon, Seattle Review, Poetry Seattle, Puget Soundings,* and *Crab Creek Review.* In 1984, she won the juried poetry competition sponsored by the *International Examiner* in Seattle. Her poems have also been anthologized in *Gathering Ground: An Anthology of Pacific Northwest Women of Color* and in *Early Ripening: American Women Poets Now.* Currently she lives in Portland, Oregon, with her husband, Charles, and her stepchildren, Sean and Anya. She keeps busy writing, painting, and being actively involved in various projects in the Oregon Buddhist Church.

Hilary Tham, poet and sumi-e artist, was born and raised in Klang, Malaysia. A graduate of the University of Malaya, she came to the United States in 1971 upon marriage to a Jewish American. She has been a tutor to Malaysian princesses, a health insurance claims reviewer, chair of the Northern Virginia Coalition to reset-tle Vietnamese refugees, president of her synagogue sisterhood, and author of five books of poetry, including *Paper Boats, Tigerbone Wine,* and *Bad Names for Women.* Her 1994 collection of poems, *Men and Other Strange Myths* (Three Continents Press), featured her art with her poems. Her most recent book is *Lane with No Name: Memoirs and Poems of a Malaysian-Chinese Girlhood* (Lynne Rienner). Recipient of artist-in-education grants from the Virginia Commission for the Arts, Tham teaches creative writing in public schools and for the Writer's Center in Bethesda, Maryland. She is editor in chief for Word Works, Inc., a nonprofit poetry press and poetry editor for *Potomac Review.* She has been featured on National Public Radio, Radio Pacifica, and cable television programs. Tham is currently working on a book-length narrative poem, *Counting,* based on her life in Buddhism, Catholicism, and Judaism.

Jora Trang is published here for the first time. Her poetry is characterized by a constant wakefulness in a world where the community is more feared than receptive. Her subjects are often silenced in the Vietnamese community—teenage pregnancy, domestic and family violence, lost legacies, and nontraditional partnerships. Trang's self-definitions are young single mother parent child woman of color artist activist. She seeks to bring poetry and the voice of women of color to performance art.

Mayli Vang, who is of Hmong ancestry, graduated from the College of Saint Catherine with a degree in English. Her poetry, fiction, and essays have appeared in *PajNtaub Voice* and *Ariston.*

Soul Choj Vang lives with his wife and daughters in Fresno, California, where he earned his M.F.A. in poetry, studying with Charles Hanzlicek and Corrine Hales. He was born in 1962 on Sky Mountain (Phu Fa), Laos, to Hmong parents. In 1976, after spending a year in the Nong Khai refugee camp in Thailand, Vang immigrated to the United States. Since then, he has lived in many parts of the U.S. and Europe and has served in the U.S. Army.

The author of *Ginseng and Other Tales from Manila* (Calyx Books, 1991), **Marianne Villanueva** was a finalist for the Manila Critics' Circle National Book Awards in 1992. She is a graduate of the Stanford University Creative Writing program and has been a 1993 California Arts Council Literature Fellow. She recently completed a residency at the Djerassi Resident Artists Program in Woodside, California, for which she received a Peninsula Community Foundation grant. Her work has appeared in numerous journals, including *Threepenny Review, Fourteen Hills,* the *Asian/Pacific-American Journal, Story Quarterly, the Literary Review,* and the *Journal of Philippine Studies.* She has been anthologized in *Flippin: Filipinos in America* (Asian American Writers' Workshop, 1996), *Into the Fire: New Asian American Prose* (Greenfield Review Press, 1996), *Songs of Ourselves: Writings by Filipino Women in English* (Anvil Press, 1995), *Charlie Chan Is Dead* (Viking Penguin, 1993), and *The Forbidden Stitch* (Calyx Books, 1989). Villanueva has recently completed a second collection of short fiction. Currently, she is a senior project adviser for the Master of Arts in Writing program at the University of San Francisco.

In 1976, **Kay Vu-Lee's** family was one of the first few Hmong groups from Laos to seek safety in Michigan. They currently live in Fresno, California, where Kay received her baccalaureate and master's degrees in English and became more familiar with her native language and people. She has coauthored "Amy Tan's 'Rules of the Game,'" in *Masterplots II: Short Story Supplement* (Salem Press, 1996); published three poems in *Oxygen,* a San Francisco quarterly; and edited and published poetry in the *Southeast Asian Newsletter* at California State University, Fresno.

Chachoua Victoria Xiong is currently a law student at Creighton School of Law. She received her M.F.A. in creative writing at Sarah Lawrence College and was an adjunct instructor of creative writing at Creighton University. Xiong was born in Laos and immigrated with her family to Nebraska when she was three years old. Her very first lesson in America was, Don't run away from a dog if you don't want it to chase you. Ms. Xiong has been published in the *International Examiner, Nebraska Journal Review,* and *Creighton Shadows.*

Mahani Zubaidy was born in Penang, Malaysia. She writes on Malaysian mammals for young and general-interest readers. She lives in Austin, Texas.